Talking Baby

Advance praise

'*Talking Baby* is required reading for every parent, grandparent, educator, student or anyone working with children. The book provides great insight into the amazing journey called "language development". Very practical with lots of tips for promoting children's language growth as well as information on the latest research in language development. I highly recommended it.'

— Elisabeth Duursma, EdD, senior lecturer in early childhood literacy, University of Wollongong

'As a mum and a linguist, I highly recommend this fabulous new book on how babies learn to talk. The authors provide fun facts and practical suggestions to parents for each developmental stage. An accessible and truly enjoyable read!'

— Dr Anita Szakay, Lecturer in Linguistics, Macquarie University, Sydney

'This is a great new book from experienced academics and researchers Maclagan and Buckley. It offers the reader a detailed yet accessible journey through the origins and subsequent unfolding of child language. The format, which includes key points "boxes", is a helpful way of summarising complex information. Readable and informative, it will be picked up by parents and students alike.'

— Dr Patricia Champion, MBE, Developmental Psychologist and Clinical Director Emeritus, The Champion Centre, Christchurch, NZ

'Although babies are "hard-wired" to learn language, Margaret Maclagan and Anne Buckley have written a highly readable and informative book. They emphasise from day one the importance on talking to newborns, laughter, simple words, reading and games through to school age. For parents who may be concerned about their child's language there is practical advice about having hearing tested and other professional help. Undoubtedly this delightful book will help parents to understand and nurture their child's natural language development.'

— Jeremy Hornibrook, Otolaryngologist and Adjunct Professor, Department of Communication Disorders, University of Canterbury, NZ

'This book is a hugely valuable addition to the literature. It is rare for a book to be so accessible and enjoyable to read, and yet so scientifically accurate and well-informed. Parents will find this a hugely enjoyable read, which encourages them to engage with, and marvel at, their child's acquisition of language. Maclagan and Buckley have provided an invaluable resource for anyone wishing to learn about the fundamentals of language development.'

— Jennifer Hay, Professor of Linguistics, University of Canterbury, and Director of the New Zealand Institute of Language, Brain and Behaviour

'This beautiful book is a joy to read – the richness of our young children learning to communicate; how to support them, how to enjoy them!'

— Dr Nikki Turner, Associate Professor, Department of General Practice and Primary Health Care, and Director, The Immunisation Advisory Centre, University of Auckland

Talking Baby

Helping your child discover language

Margaret Maclagan
& Anne Buckley

FINCH PUBLISHING
SYDNEY

To our mothers, fathers and all the interested adults in our early lives who helped us to discover our language.

Ialking Baby: How to help your child discover language

First published in 2016 in Australia and New Zealand by Finch Publishing Pty Limited, ABN 49 057 285 248, Suite 2207, 4 Daydream Street, Warriewood, NSW, 2102, Australia.

16   8 7 6 5 4 3 2 1

There is a National Library of Australia Cataloguing-in-Publication entry available at the National Library.

Edited by Karen Gee
Editorial assistance by Megan English
Text designed and typeset in Utopia by Meg Dunworth
Cover design by Jo Hunt
Printed by Griffin Press

The paper used to produce this book is a natural, recyclable product made from wood grown in sustainable plantation forests. The manufacturing processes conform to the environmental regulations in the country of origin.

Finch titles can be viewed and purchased at **www.finch.com.au**

Contents

About this book

The baby brain is an incredible learning machine.
Its future – to a great extent – is in our hands.

—National Geographic, January 2015 (p. 76)

People used to learn about what is normal in language development by watching older members of their extended families interacting with young children. Now with smaller families, people often learn by reading instead. This book is written primarily for parents, but also for grandparents, for those living or working with young children, and for those who are simply curious about language and the way it's learnt. It takes a child-led approach to encouraging language development.

Throughout the book we'll use 'they', 'them' and 'their' to refer to your baby or young child to avoid 'he' or 'she'. We'll also give ages when language developments usually happen, but all ages are approximate and can vary by *at least* six months in either direction. Language development is just like motor development: a milestone like running, which usually occurs at about eighteen months, can occur as early as twelve months or as late as 24 months and still be well within the normal developmental range. Similarly first words, which usually appear by about twelve months, can appear anywhere from nine to twenty months.

This book describes in detail language development for English-speaking children. It was written in, but is not restricted to, an Australasian context. Many of the patterns of language development described here will also apply to other languages and cultures, especially the development of early sounds and meanings.

The books we suggest in the various chapters and at the end are well-known children's books that are readily available in libraries and bookshops – they're meant as examples of useful books you could use rather than a prescription of what you should go out and buy.

How the book is organised

Chapters 1 to 6 describe your baby's language development, alongside their physical development, until your baby is about eighteen months old. After this time, language development becomes much more complicated – too much is happening for us to be able to keep describing everything developmentally, so the structure of the book changes from Chapter 7 onwards.

If you've ever tried to learn another language you'll know how many different things there are to learn. You need to learn the words, the sounds, how the words fit together and all sorts of information about what you should and shouldn't say to particular people. As your baby learns English, they've got to learn just as much. They have to learn the words and sounds of English. They have to learn how to put the words together and they have to learn how to use what they've learnt. For example, they'll learn that they can talk in one way with their friends but that they need to talk differently with their grandparents.

Each of the chapters in the rest of the book explores a specific area of language. In Chapter 7 we'll talk about play, because play is the way young children learn. In chapters 8, 9 and 10 we'll explore just how much your child will be able to do with their language even when they can use just one word at a time. Chapter 8 will focus on their very early words, Chapter 9 will look at how they use these words and Chapter 10 explores the sorts of things they talk about.

Chapter 11 covers the exciting development that happens when your child can put two words together and Chapter 12 looks at the more complicated things they can then talk about. Chapters 13 and 14 talk about the development of the sounds of English and the pattern of errors and progress your child is likely to show.

Chapters 15 and 16 move into more specific areas of language development. Chapter 17 then takes language out from the home into the world and Chapter 18 looks at some special topics like colour and number development. Chapter 19 gives answers to some common questions and, to end, Chapter 20 looks at some common problems with speech and language development.

We hope you enjoy discovering more about how language grows and ways you can choose to nourish its development in the young children in your life.

1.

Overview:
What can they do?

The table on the next page gives a general overview of speech and language milestones for children from birth to five years. Although the main focus in this book is on babies and young children, It's useful to see the progression of language development throughout the preschool years so we've included milestones up to age five. All the ages in this table are a general guide, and individual children vary greatly. Children will progress through these stages at different rates. At any particular time, your child may be a bit ahead or a bit behind other children of their age. This usually doesn't matter, but if you have any concerns, *always* seek another opinion.

Table 1: **Speech and language milestones**

	How they respond	What they say
Birth to 6 weeks	• Startles at loud sounds. • Quietens when spoken to. • Seems to recognise your voice and quietens if crying.	• Makes pleasure sounds (cooing, from about 3 weeks). • Smiles when sees you (from about 6 weeks). • Makes a string of repetitive sounds – at first mainly aa-aa-aa or other vowel sounds.
6 weeks to 6 months	• Moves eyes in direction of sounds. • Responds to changes in the tone of your voice.	• Smiles when they see you (from about 6 weeks). • Begins to 'take a turn' in 'conversation', initially by a movement, grimace or a sound after you speak to them (2–3 months). • Babbling sounds more speech-like, with different consonant sounds – bababa, mumumum. • Chuckles and laughs. • Plays with the pitch of sounds (the melody of the voice) by making sounds that go up and down.
6 months to 12 months	• Enjoys games like peek-a-boo and clap hands. • Turns and looks in the direction of sounds. • Listens when you speak to them. • Recognises words for common items like 'bottle', 'shoe', 'hat' or 'ball'. • Starts to respond to requests (e.g. 'Come here' or 'Want more?').	• Babbling is more varied e.g., badaba (9–10 months). • Uses speech or non-crying sounds to get and keep attention. • Uses gestures to communicate (puts arms up to ask you to pick them up). • Says 'bye bye' with a wave, 'peek-a-boo' when hiding their face (these 'performatives' occur before the first true words; the sound and gesture always go together).

How you can help	See these chapters	
• Talk to your baby as much as possible. • It doesn't matter what you say, as long as you're talking. • Imitate their sounds back to them. • Exaggerate the melody of your voice and use lots of facial expression as you talk to them. • Sing simple, repetitive songs to them.	*Chapter* 3	Birth to 6 weeks
• Imitate their babble sounds as much as you can. • Hold conversations, where anything they do is their turn. • It still doesn't matter what you say, because they won't understand the content. • They will understand the tone of your voice. • Keep singing to them. They won't mind if you aren't a super star.	Chapter 4	6 weeks to 6 months
• Still imitate as much of their babble sounds as you can, even non-English sounds. • Imitate their gestures and say what you're doing. • When they put their arms up to be picked up, put your arms out and say 'You want to come up?' Then pick them up and say 'Up you come'. • Imitate their waving or clapping and play peek-a-boo with them. • Try making simple requests like 'Come here' or 'Get your slippers'. If they don't respond, it doesn't matter, but you may be surprised.	Chapter 5	6 months to 12 months

Table 1: **Speech and language milestones continued**

	How they respond	What they say
12 months to 18 months	• Points to a few body parts when asked and to pictures in a book when named. • Follows simple directions ('get your cup'). • May only do these things when they want to, not when you want them to. • Understands simple questions ('Where's your hat?'). • Enjoys simple songs and rhymes.	• Around first birthday has one or two words ('hi', 'dog', 'dada', 'mama'), although sounds may not be clear. • Real words may be said alongside babble or may be heard after a babble-free period of a month or more. • Produces strings of jargon (nonsense words) that sound like your speech. • Uses 'giant' words (e.g. 'gimme', 'look at') that are only one word, even though they sound like two words.
18 months to 2 years	• Enjoys 'reading' picture books without words. • Usually follows two-step commands ('Get your ball and give it to Daddy', 'Find your slippers and bring them to me'). • May not respond to you if they're too involved in what they're doing.	• Has words for lots of different things such as names for animals, clothing, toys, foods, body parts. • Has words for different meaning categories e.g. 'hot' (description), 'up' (action), 'gone' (non-existence), 'no!' (rejection). • May use chains of single words before putting two words together: 'Door. Open.' or 'Cat. Gone.' • Puts two words together ('More (ba)nana', 'No juice', 'Mummy book') – this will happen when your child has learnt about fifty words. • Uses some one- or two-word questions ('Where ball?' 'Go Nanna?' '(A)nother bickie?'). • Speech is mostly understood by close family members. • Uses different consonant sounds at the beginning of words. • You'll notice more errors in your child's speech because they're saying more.

How you can help	See these chapters	
• Say their first words back to them, but don't imitate the cute way they say them. • Work out a strategy for when you don't understand their strings of jargon – 'You show me' often works. • Play interactive games: stacking blocks together (and knocking them down), rolling a ball to each other. • Say what you are doing as you do it. • Name body parts: when you're changing their nappy, point out their toes and belly button. • Play interactive nursery rhymes and songs. • Ask them to do simple things such as getting their shoes; they may not always do them, but sometimes they will.	First words are in Chapter 6 Nonsense sounds are in Chapter 6 Play and language are in Chapter 7 Early words are in Chapter 8 Early uses of language are in Chapter 9	12 months to 18 months
• Talk about the pictures in books. • Don't read the words in books unless the story is very short or has strong rhyme and rhythm. • If they want to, play the 'Wassat?' naming game where you ask them 'What's that?' • They may ask you 'What's that?' about things they know so they can answer their own question; not all children do this. • Repeat their two-word 'sentences' adding in something extra – 'Where kitty?' 'Where's kitty? Kitty's hiding.' • Don't copy their cute pronunciations but repeat what they say with the correct pronunciation. 'Dere dod.' 'Yes, there's the dog'. • Don't try to make them imitate the correct pronunciation – they'll get there in time. • Sing nursery rhymes or songs even though they may not join in yet. • Leave pauses so they can fill in key words in favourite stories or songs. • *An increase in errors is a sign of progress, so don't worry.*	Early words are in Chapter 8 Early meaning categories are in Chapters 8 and 10 The 'Wassat?' game is in Chapters 9 and 16 Putting two words together is in Chapter 11 Sound development is in Chapters 13 and 14	18 months to 2 years

Table 1: **Speech and language milestones continued**

	How they respond	What they say
2 years to 3 years	• Understands differences in meaning ('go-stop,' 'in-out,' 'big-little,' 'up-down'). • Follows two-step requests ('Get the car and put it in the toy box'), including ones where there aren't clues in the situation to tell them what to do ('Find your ball and put it under the cushion'). • Listens to longer stories. • Likes stories with strong rhymes.	• Has a word for most things. • Uses two or three words to talk about things or ask for them. • Uses m, n, p, b, h, w, and f sounds. • Familiar listeners understand most of your child's speech most of the time. • Only about half your child's speech is understood by strangers. • Can count two objects.
3 years to 4 years	• Hears you when you call from another room. • Hears television or radio at the same volume level as other family members. • Answers simple 'who?', 'what?' and 'where?' questions. • May answer simple 'why?' questions.	• Can tell you some of what they did at preschool or at friends' homes. • People outside of the family usually understand your child's speech. • By 4 years is almost always understood. • Uses sentences that have four or more words.
4 years to 5 years	• Pays attention to a short story and answers simple questions about it. • Hears and understands most of what is said at home and preschool.	• Uses sentences that give lots of details. • Tells stories that stick to topic, but may not yet be in the order you expect. • Communicates easily with others. • Says most sounds correctly except a few, such as l, s, r, v, z, ch, sh, th. • May say rhyming words. • May name some letters and numbers. • Uses the same grammar as the rest of the family. • Talks differently in different situations – has an 'inside' and an 'outside' voice. • Has a working vocabulary of up to 6000 words (at 5 years). • May start to tell 'jokes' but won't understand the punch line.

How you can help	See these chapters	
• Comment on opposites – 'Daddy is big, Elliot is little'. • Ask them to do things for you – put the cup or plate on the kitchen bench, go and get their hat; sometimes they'll do it. • Play interactive games – train sets or doll's houses lead to lots of language. • Sing nursery rhymes or other songs and wait for them to fill in the last line.	Vocabulary development is in Chapters 10 and 12 Putting two words together is in Chapter 11 Sound development is in Chapters 13 and 14 Opposites are in Chapters 12 and 17 Saying 'no!' is in Chapter 15 Counting is in Chapter 18	2 years to 3 years
• Play more complex games – train sets can have complicated stories added to the action, and dolls can go to birthday parties or shopping. • Ask them what they did at preschool and try to make sense of what they say. • Still talk about the pictures rather than reading the words in long books. • Comment on colours, but don't expect them to get them right.	Question development is in Chapters 15 and 16 Colours are in Chapter 18 Different language for different situations is in Chapter 17 Remembering what they did earlier is in Chapter 18	3 years to 4 years
• Start to read the words in stories, but still not all the words in long stories. • Read and re-read their favourite stories. • Ask questions to sort out what they mean when they try to tell you something complicated. • If they want to, play rhyming games. • If they are interested, comment on the names of letters and numbers. • Don't correct their pronunciation, but don't imitate their cute errors.	Listening to a story is in Chapter 17 Tells stories is in Chapter 17 Later sound development is in Chapter 14 Letters and numbers are in Chapter 18 Jokes are in Chapter 17	4 years to 5 years

2.

Beginnings

The sun streams in through the French doors on the north side of the living room. It's warm enough to play outside but much easier to keep track of this staggering one-year-old inside for the time being. I have the job of occupying this little guy and distracting him from the fact that his mother is out of the room. He is happy for the moment but I need to keep his attention. He has always adored birds. I point out the window and call his name. 'Look at the birds. They're eating the bread. Look at the birds on the lawn. Lots of birds. How many are there? One bird … two birds.'

He is watching the birds intently and just when I think he has lost interest, he reaches out towards the window and I hear him say 'ber'. It is, I am sure, his first word. I check with his mother when she returns. Is it a word, she wonders? If so, it is his first one. I confirm it with her. Yes, he was definitely pointing and meaning 'bird' when he said it. We smile and laugh. He is 'talking'! A first milestone has been reached.

It is the beginning … of something awesome. By the time this little boy is at school, like children throughout the world, he will be talking pretty much like the people in his community.

A staggering achievement

By school age your child will:

- speak your language and have a working vocabulary of up to 6000 words
- form complete and complex sentences, describing their world and instructing those in it
- produce almost every sound in their language reasonably correctly
- be ready to learn new and abstract ideas through their own and others' use of language
- be ready to learn to represent language through written words (reading and writing)
- be ready to learn maths.

The development of language through the preschool years is a remarkable journey. But it is not one that your child will make alone. Children make this journey because people around them talked to them while they were a baby and then kept right on talking.

When things go wrong: Genie the Wild Child

There is sad and compelling evidence that children who are not talked to don't learn to talk and communicate with others.

One of the best-studied and best-reported cases is that of Genie, the so-called Wild Child. Locked away in isolation from infancy, her only contact through childhood was with an abusive father who spoke to her mostly in 'barks and growls'. Genie was hit with a wooden spoon whenever she uttered a sound. At the age of fourteen when she was rescued by her mother and taken to hospital, she had the language and motor skills of a baby. She could say only a few words including 'stopit' and 'nomore'.

Genie was keen to communicate using gesture, and did learn some language over time with intensive specialist input. She could utter some simple sentences. However, she never fully mastered English, as almost all five-year-olds in the English-speaking world do with ease. Children may be hardwired to learn language, as research indicates, but they still need to hear lots of language and have an opportunity to put it into use to become proficient speakers.

⚛ WHAT DOES SCIENCE TELL US?

Lots of talk

Families that talk a lot also talk about more different things. They use more varied sentences, a greater range of words, and more of their conversations are on topics the child initiates. These were some of the findings of a major study that looked at 1300 hours of casual interaction between parents and their young children. The study findings and subsequent work inspired by it are the basis for recent early intervention initiatives in the United States.

3.

A sea of sound

Up to six weeks

First words may mark your baby's beginning as a talker, but they are not their first beginnings as a communicator. Anyone who has spent time with young babies will know how effective a communication tool a baby's cry is! Even in early infancy, babies know a lot more about communication than we may think. From the very beginning, they are busy learning how to have conversations.

Babies cry

- The one-day-old baby is hungry, so she cries.
- The one-week-old baby is wet and uncomfortable, so he cries.
- The ten-day-old baby has a sore tummy, so he cries.
- The two-week-old baby is overtired and having trouble going to sleep, so she cries.

At first, the only way babies can communicate is by crying. The amazing thing is that as a parent you can usually sort out what's wrong and what your baby wants when they cry – but often only for your own baby. When mothers used to stay in the maternity ward for several days after giving birth, they could rapidly recognise whose baby was crying and only that mother would head off to see what the problem was.

What can newborn babies hear?

Although newborn babies can't make a lot of different sounds to communicate with, they are surprisingly good at hearing speech. Babies can't see before they're born but they can hear. Sounds are muffled, but one-day-old babies still recognise their mother's voice.

They can also recognise some speech sounds – they can hear the difference between 'ba' and 'da' but not between 'oo' and 'aa'. And the same is true for one-month-old babies. Babies up to six months old can distinguish between sounds that are not in the language they will learn – but by eleven months, when they are actually starting to learn their own language, they can no longer recognise sounds that don't form part of that language.

It looks as if our brains really are specifically hardwired to learn language. But young chinchillas can also distinguish between these sounds – so maybe human babies aren't quite so special. However, even if babies aren't uniquely hardwired to learn language, these abilities sure make it easier for them to learn it!

The power of a mother's voice

Researchers got babies to suck on a dummy until they'd settled into a nice, regular rhythm. Then a sound was played, and the babies started sucking faster because the sound was new and interesting. The sound was played continuously until their sucking slowed down again, and then another sound was played. If the baby recognised that the new sound was different, they sucked faster for a while, and if it sounded the same they kept sucking at the same regular rate.

Babies also sucked faster for longer when listening to their mother's voice than when listening to other voices. This shows that they can recognise their mother's voice from other voices, and that they prefer it.

Why talk to newborn babies?

If sounds are muffled before a baby is born, what can they actually hear? And is there any point in reading to them or talking specifically to them? The main thing they'll hear is the *rhythm* of your voice. And they'll hear the speech melody, the way your voice goes up and down as you talk – there's no need to exaggerate or to make your voice more sing-song, your own voice patterns will be quite distinctive enough. Being pregnant is a perfect excuse to talk to yourself – you're letting your baby hear your voice! A wonderful way to counteract 'baby brain'.

If you've developed the habit of talking to yourself before your baby's born it'll be easier to keep it up once they've actually arrived. Once babies are born it's *really* important to talk to them. Many parents feel uncomfortable talking to a small baby who obviously doesn't understand what they're saying. The fact that you're tired much of the time just makes things worse. But even though babies don't 'understand', they're still learning a lot. They're learning to focus on the human voice.

What language will they learn?

Newborn babies would rather listen to the human voice than to other sounds, and as you talk to your baby they're learning to pay attention to you. And they're hearing lots of the language they're going to learn.

Although babies are born with an ability to learn language, they're not born with an ability to learn a *particular* language. So a small Chinese baby brought up by English-speaking parents in an English-speaking environment will speak perfect English – and the reverse is also true. An English baby brought up by Chinese-speaking parents in a Chinese-speaking environment will learn perfect Mandarin. That's a skill we lose quite early. If you try to learn another language after puberty (and probably even earlier) you'll almost inevitably end up with a marked accent.

Small babies are totally focused on their own needs – they have to be in order to survive! As you talk to your very young baby, you're letting them hear their native language. But you're also 'teaching' them how to interact. You're not consciously teaching them, and they're not consciously learning, but how to interact is one of the things small babies need to learn. And as you talk to them and interact with them, they slowly learn to focus outside themselves.

The original language?

There's a story about an ancient king who wanted to discover the first ever language. So he put two babies in the care of a shepherd who was forbidden to talk to them, to see what they would say. (You can instantly see the problem here. Babies need to hear language in order to learn it.) Eventually the babies said something that sounded a bit like 'bekos', the Phrygian word for bread. So the king decided that Phrygian was the very first language.

More to say: ideas for parents ⓦ

- **Talk to your baby.** Some parents seem to know instinctively what to say to a small baby – what to talk about. But many don't and feel uncomfortable trying. The good news is that it doesn't matter what you say to a small baby – so long as you're talking.

- **Talk about anything.** Talk about the weather, about whether it's a nice day or cold and miserable. Talk about what you're going to do, then what you're actually doing, then what you've done – yes, it can be as repetitive as that! If you're doing something that takes a while you can have a 'conversation' with your baby.

- **Leave time for your baby's 'response'.** Let your baby have a turn. Say something to them, then wait a few seconds for them to make a sound or do something like waving their arms. Then say something more, and then wait again.

- **Anything the baby does is their 'turn' in the 'conversation'.** It doesn't matter what their 'turn' is, it doesn't have to be a sound. A movement is fine. A burp, a grimace, hand or leg movements, so long as they've actually done something – that's their part in 'talking' to you. If you have these 'conversations' often enough, your baby will learn that people take turns in a conversation.

- **Make eye contact and exaggerate facial expressions.** You can use body language to indicate to the baby that it is their turn to say something. One way is to get eye contact with them or wait until they look at you. Or open your eyes wide or lift your eyebrows to show that you expect something from them. Any movement or sound from them counts as their turn. You might respond with some words such as 'What are you doing?' And then in response to the next 'turn' from the baby you might say, 'I think it's time for you to have your bath.' And then a question: 'Are you ready for your bath?' And so on as you continue the 'conversation'.

💬 Talking point

When you're changing your baby's nappy, the 'conversation' might go something like this, with pauses (...) left for your baby's 'response':

We're going to change your nappy ...
Here's your room, and here's your change table ...
Let's put you on your change table ...
and unzip your onesie ...
and get this leg out ...
Here are your toes ...
And now let's take this messy nappy off ...
and clean you up ...
Bye-bye nappy! ...
And now you're all clean ...
So let's put a clean nappy on ...
And put your toes back in and zip you up ...
And now you're all ready to go again.

Another perfect time for commenting is when your baby is in a bouncer. Each time they bounce you say something – then if they make a sound, that's their turn in the conversation, or their bounce is their turn. As you talk to your baby you're not consciously 'teaching' them, but they're certainly learning how to 'converse' with you.

Summary of tips

- Talk to your baby!
- Talk about anything.
- Leave time for your baby's 'response'.
- Anything the baby does is their 'turn' in the 'conversation'.
- Make eye contact and exaggerate facial expressions.

4.

Talking by accident

Six weeks to six months

Although crying is a really effective way for babies to get their needs met, language experts don't think that language develops out of babies' early cries. Adults still cry as well as talk – often we seem to have as little choice about crying as a small baby does. And crying is often as effective for us as it is for a baby. But crying isn't very useful for talking to people.

Cooing sounds

So if language doesn't develop out of crying, where does it come from? After a few weeks, babies start to produce different sorts of sounds. About the time your baby starts to smile, you'll notice they're no longer just crying all the time. They're starting to make little cooing noises when they're comfortable – often after a feed. A six- to seven-week-old baby will focus on your face and 'talk' to you, often in a long string of 'aa' sounds. There'll probably be some consonant-like sounds as well, often sounds made in the back of the throat, that aren't part of English. It can be a really long 'conversation' – a long string of 'aa' vowels plus an occasional consonant. And when you reply, they'll have another turn.

This sort of 'conversation' is usually rewarding for both you and your baby – you feel special because they're focusing totally on you, and they feel special because they're getting your full attention. And it's so nice when they're cooing at you rather than crying at the top of their lungs!

Not all babies smile at the same time and nor do they all coo at the same time, but smiling and cooing often occur at about the same age. That's something we'll see a lot as we look at the way babies develop language – there are often motor and language milestones that seem to occur together.

⚛ WHAT DOES SCIENCE TELL US?

Where did language come from?

Some parts of our language may have developed from birdsong – at least that is what some researchers think. This view was first put forward as early as 1871 by Charles Darwin.

Birds like the nightingale can produce as many as 100 to 200 different melodies. They use their songs to communicate with each other, with each song being a single message.

Like birdsong, human speech is melodic and can be put together in different uttered combinations. The researchers suggest that people may first have had the ability to sing and that this developed over time into the language we use today. Perhaps this explains why singing is so enjoyable to so many of us.

Your baby's early sounds

The vowel-like sounds at this cooing stage are reasonably like your language, but why are the consonants often so strange? It's because your baby's tongue is relatively larger than your tongue. It takes up more of the space inside their mouth, and touches the roof of the mouth in all sorts of odd places. And because small babies are often lying on their backs, or supported at a very shallow angle (as in a bouncer), their tongue often makes contact with the back of the throat and so they make those strange sounds. It's all part of learning to talk.

At first, all the consonant-like sounds a baby makes are accidental. They just happen when the tongue touches the roof of the mouth and the baby can't make them deliberately. You might think this isn't the case, because babies can get into a rhythm and repeat the same sounds over and over again in the one 'conversation' or even over one day – but the next conversation or the next day, they're usually making different sounds.

In this 'accidental' period, your baby will often experiment with other types of sounds rather than just sounds made with their tongue. They may make trills with their lips or blow raspberries. Since it's during this period from six weeks to six months that many babies are moving onto solid food, blowing raspberries with a mouth full of food is great fun – for your baby, if not for you!

⚛ What does science tell us?

Why we laugh

Research into laughter shows it's not as much about humour as it is about relationships. Babies first laugh at about three to four months old and use laughter before they can talk to interact with their parents and others. It's thought that laughter evolved from the panting behaviour of our ape ancestors. Apes laugh in response to tickling, rough-and-tumble play and chasing games just as humans do.

The melody of speech

Often just before six months there's an important development that people usually don't even notice. Your baby may start playing with pitch patterns, the melodies of speech. Sometimes they go up and other times they go down, but they start to really play with the range of pitches they can make. This is important because we use pitch patterns to tell other people what's really important in what we've just said. We might say '*John* ate the cake' with stress and a higher pitch on 'John' to mean that John, and not someone else, ate it; but if we say 'John *ate* the cake' we mean that he ate it, rather than buying it or doing something else with it. From about five months on, your baby will start to play with the pitch patterns they will use when they start to really talk. It's one of those important language milestones and deserves to be celebrated, but it often goes completely unnoticed.

The same but different

A group of boys is playing an informal game of cricket. Jack hits a high shot. 'I've got it,' yells Tony, but it slips through his fingers. 'You silly idiot,' yells Zane, and everyone laughs.

A group of men is playing cards. Bill misses an easy trick. 'You silly idiot,' yells Don. There's a tense silence.

Same words, different pitch patterns, different tone of voice, different effect.

Readers were listeners first

Your baby isn't ready to read yet but it's never too early to lay the groundwork for reading. If you want to help your child read when they're older, talk to them a lot from a young age. There's a lot of research that stresses the impact of early language learning on how well children do at school. One study followed babies from seven months to the age of three. It found that different families use incredibly different amounts of language with their children. The more language the children heard, the better their own language was by the time they reached three years of age. When the children were older, the number of words they knew at age three was a direct predictor of their language skills at age nine to ten. And the more words they knew, the better they understood what they were reading.

So what you do right now is crucial. The more you talk to your baby, the better chance you give them for later reading and learning.

> ### 💬 Talking point
>
> Your baby smiles at you and waves their arms.
> You might say, 'You're awake!'
> They hiccup.
> You might say, 'Oh, what a noise! Have you got hiccups?'
> And so the 'conversation' continues.

More to say: ideas for parents 💡

🌶 **Talk to your baby!** As your baby 'talks' to you, so you talk back – it still doesn't matter what you say because they can't yet really understand you. What matters is that you say *something*. We know a mother who really wasn't comfortable talking to her small baby. So she said multiplication tables to him – with lovely rhythm. She'd stop and give him time to take a 'turn' – kicking his legs or waving his arms or smiling, and then carry on until it was time for him to have another turn. He had her full attention and heard her voice with its own distinctive quality, pitch patterns and rhythm. And he was learning to take turns. Also talk to your baby when you're in the car, especially if you want to keep them awake.

🌶 **Sing nursery rhymes.** Don't forget nursery rhymes, spoken or sung. Don't worry if you can't sing – your baby will be a wonderfully uncritical audience. It's also amazing how often singing will quieten a fractious baby when talking won't.

One good time to use nursery rhymes is when you're changing your baby. Say, 'Round and round the garden like a teddy bear,' as you tickle them round their belly button or 'This little piggy went to market,' on each toe before you put their clothes back on; 'This little horse goes trot a trot,' then 'This little horse goes gallopy,' as you hold them on your knee afterwards. Action rhymes like these are wonderful for your baby. Feel free to make up your own.

- **Use your baby's name.** When you're talking to your baby, use their name to get their attention. Putting their name into a nursery rhyme helps keep their attention: 'Twinkle twinkle little star, How I wonder what you are, Up above the world so high, Like a *Jenny* in the sky ...'

- **Play turn-taking games.** Rhymes and games can be another fun way for babies to begin learning how 'conversations' work. Turn-taking games like peek-a-boo are excellent for 'conversations'. Hide your face from your baby when you know they're looking at you and then after a short moment say 'boo'. This game can be played endlessly! You'll get tired of it long before they will.

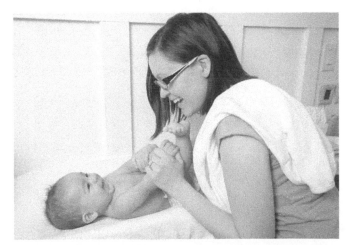

Another turn-taking game

Another game is *Jack in the box*. Hold your baby firmly on your knee while saying the words. Then lift them up high after the last line and say 'up'.

> Jack in the box, Jack in the box, quiet and still.
> Will I come out? Will I come out?
> [Pause]
> Yes, I will.

Humpty Dumpty can also be used as a 'conversation'.

> Humpty Dumpty sat on a wall [with the baby sitting on
>   your lap facing you]
> Humpty Dumpty had a great fall [move the baby back as if
>   gently falling and then bring them back upright again]
> All the king's horses and all the king's men
> Couldn't put Humpty together again.

After a couple of times, pause before the 'fall' and let your baby show they anticipate the fall by laughing or through body language. After the rhyme, pause and then put the baby's response into words: 'More?' or 'No more?'

📖 Talking and reading times

Any time is a good time to read to a small child. It's never too early to start reading to them. It's really good to start reading when they're very small to begin the habit of focusing together. They won't understand a story yet but they'll enjoy the rhythm of your voice and your undivided attention.

Three things are important when reading to your baby:

- Read stories with strong rhythm and rhyme. This helps your baby focus on your voice.
- Read stories you enjoy. Even though your baby won't understand it yet, they'll somehow know if you don't like the story.
- Share simple books with your baby. It's good if you've got some cloth or cardboard books that they can hold themselves – and it doesn't matter if they're upside down.

Summary of tips

- Talk to your baby!
- Sing nursery rhymes.
- Use your baby's name.
- Play turn-taking games.
- Any time is a good time to read to a small child.
- Read stories with strong rhythm and rhyme.
- Read stories that you enjoy.
- Share simple books with your baby.

5.

Are they talking yet?

Six months to twelve months

So far your baby hasn't had much control over what they say. But at about six to seven months, this starts to change. At this age, babies start to gain control over their tongue. Their head has grown and their tongue takes up less space in their mouth so it can be moved around with more precision. About six months old babies also start to sit up – another example of language and motor developments occurring at about the same age. Some babies can sit by themselves by this age. Others still need to be propped up. But most babies can be vertical for some of the time, and this is important for language because it means the tongue isn't just flopping against the back of the mouth.

Family names

Many languages use 'b', 'd', 'm' and 'n' sounds that children learn very early for close family names:

- English has 'baby', 'mummy', 'daddy' and 'nanna'
- French has *bébé* ('baby') and *maman* ('mummy')
- Russian has *babushka* ('grandmother') and *mama* ('mother')
- German has *papa* ('daddy') and *mama* or *mutter* ('mother').

Somewhere in the history of language, people imitated babies' early babble sounds and shaped them into these important words. It sure makes it easier for babies to learn them.

First sounds

Around this time your baby will start to produce repeated sounds like 'ba ba ba'. Usually the first consonant they have control over is 'b', which is nice and easy for them to make because this sound is made with both lips. Usually the first vowel is 'a' because the tongue just has to be low in the mouth. And everyone says, 'Oh he's talking – he said, "baby" to me' even though the child is not saying real words yet. Margaret's mother swore that she talked at six months 'because you looked at me and smiled and said "baby", dear.' It wasn't actually a 'real' word yet but Margaret couldn't convince her mother of that.

✹ WHAT DOES SCIENCE TELL US?

Babies' brains hard at work

A baby's brain is engaged in trying to talk right from the beginning. The brains of seven-month-old babies are already trying to figure out how to make the right movements to produce words.

This was the incredible finding of a recent study using brain scanning technology. The study looked at what was happening in the motor areas of the brain when babies were only listening and not actually producing any sounds. As expected, there was activity in one of the listening areas of the brain (the superior temporal gyrus). But there was also activity in the areas where motor movements for speech are planned (Broca's area and the cerebellum). Even though the babies couldn't yet deliberately produce sounds, this study showed their brains were hard at work learning how to make them.

Early babble

Even though it's not really 'talking', your baby's babble is nearly as important as their first 'real' words. It means that your baby is learning to control their tongue and lips so that soon they'll be able to make real words. But first they need a lot of practice with just making sounds in a controlled way – in repetitive babble.

Most babies start with 'ba ba ba' but some start with 'ma ma ma', another consonant made using the lips. This is usually followed by 'da da da' or 'na na na' and a bit later by 'ga ga ga'. And just as 'ba ba ba' doesn't mean 'baby', so 'ma ma ma' doesn't mean 'mummy' and 'da da da' doesn't mean 'daddy'. No matter what language the baby is going to learn, they still make these same repetitive babble sounds. Even deaf babies do this – it seems to be a motor practice thing.

Somewhere in this period, 'da da da' often becomes associated with Daddy – much to his delight. But to the chagrin of many mothers, 'ma ma ma' often seems to mean, 'I'm miserable. Look after me, Mummy.' And for many children, 'na na na' can end up being a food word, because bananas are such a good early food.

Varied babble

At first, all of your baby's babble will consist of the same sounds – it will always be 'ba ba ba' or 'da da da'. But somewhere around nine or ten months of age most babies start to use varied babble. Instead of only saying 'ba ba ba' or 'ma ma ma' they might also say 'ba da ba' or 'ma ma ga ga'. This shows they're gaining still more control over their tongue. And this varied babble is important because, although deaf babies produce ordinary babble, they don't usually produce varied babble. And they don't usually experiment with pitch patterns either (see the section on the melody of speech in Chapter 4 for playing with pitch patterns). So once your baby starts to do these things it's a good indication that they're both hearing – and listening.

Performatives

You'd expect the next stage to be the first true words. But before real words appear there are often what are known as performatives, where a word is associated with a gesture so it is 'performed'. The two most common early performatives are 'bye' together with a (usually very small) hand wave and 'clap' as your baby claps their hands. Because the words do not appear without the gestures – or the gestures without the words – they are performatives rather than real words, but they do show that your baby is well on the way to talking. Another performative for some young children is 'peek-a-boo' (often said as 'peepoh' or just 'boo') as they hide their face and reappear.

Your role is to model waving and clapping for your baby and to wave and clap back to them as they say the words. Some babies will simply say the word while others will only do the action, but eventually most will say the words 'bye' and 'clap' as they do the appropriate actions. And again, the most important thing you need to do is to keep talking to them.

Now the stage is set for the first real words to appear!

> ### ⌯ Talking point
> Your baby says 'Bye' as they wave.
> You might say 'Bye-bye Daddy. Daddy's going in the car. Bye-bye.'

Increasing understanding

Some time in this babbling period you'll realise that your baby is understanding much more than they did earlier in their life. It's even more important to talk to a babbling baby than earlier on, but if you've been saying or singing nonsense words or, as in our earlier example multiplication tables, just so your baby can hear you talking, this doesn't seem such a good idea once they start to understand.

On the other hand, if you *have* been talking to your baby, you'll be less self-conscious by now and you'll probably be comfortable commenting about what is happening around you both. It's good to comment on anything that both you and your baby can see – it doesn't really matter what, just so long as both of you can see or hear it. Babies react to sudden noises so if you hear any noises it's good to comment on them as well.

✺ WHAT DOES SCIENCE TELL US?

Sharing books grows language

A study showed that shared reading between parents and infants at eight months of age was related to children's language abilities at twelve months. This was particularly true for girls. The language of children who had shared reading with their parents at eight months was still advanced at sixteen months.

Looking at things together

Somewhere in this period you'll notice a change in the way your baby is looking at things. At first they'll be totally focused on you and your face, and you'll be focused on them. This is what's called *reciprocal gaze* – you're both looking at each other. But one day you'll realise that rather than looking at each other, you're both looking at something else – the cat or a toy, or Grandad who is coming into the room. This is called *joint reference gaze* – you're both looking at something else together. And it's very important for language development.

It's essential for bonding that mother (or father or other caregiver) and baby look at each other, but it's essential for learning that you can both look at something else. Then, when your baby has enough words you'll both be able to talk about it. Once you and your baby can both look at the same thing, you can point to something and they'll look at it. This is something we don't even think about as parents – it seems so obvious. But it's really important for learning.

In contrast, try pointing out something to your cat. Margaret finally learnt that it was no good pointing to her cat's food bowl to tell him he'd been fed; she actually had to touch the bowl, otherwise the cat only looked at her finger. Similarly, young babies look at your finger. But older babies start to look in the direction you're pointing – and you can start to discover the world together. If your baby touches an object, you can take it as a request for that object or perhaps an attempt to show you something. It's helpful if you give it to them or touch it, name it or comment on it. Or a combination of all of these.

More to say: ideas for parents ♀

- **Imitate your baby.** At this stage, if you can imitate what your baby is saying, do! You may be amazed at the strange sounds you can produce. Over this babbling period, babies often make sounds that won't be part of the language they'll eventually learn. For instance, some babies love to make trills like the Scottish 'r' sound made with the tip of the tongue or the French 'r' that's made with the uvular at the back of the throat. Neither of these sounds is part of our English speech; they're just fun for your baby to make.

  It's good if your baby hears you repeating as much as you can of what they're saying. And somewhere around ten months of age or so they may try to imitate you back. So you imitate them, and then they imitate you and you get a lovely circular interaction going. Not all babies imitate like this, but it's fun if they do.

- **Ask them to do simple things.** Towards the end of this babbling period you may find that your baby can follow simple commands such as taking a toy to Nanna if you're all in the room together. This is something that parents often don't think to do with their first child – it happens automatically with second and later children, because they're asked to do things in the same way that their older brothers and sisters are and often to their parents' surprise they do what they're asked.

- **Sing to them.** Simple, repetitive action songs are good, especially ones where the child can join in the action. With a song like, *If you're happy and you know it clap your hands*, you'll probably find that at first you have to help your child clap their hands or do the other actions. Eventually they'll start to do the actions on their own, but it may take a while. They may also start to join in the animal sounds in songs like, *Old Macdonald had a Farm.*

♥ **Talk about what they're looking at.** In this period, it still doesn't matter so much what you say as long as you keep talking. If possible, make it relevant to what's happening around you right now and be sure that your baby is looking at what you're talking about.

📖 Talking and reading times

'Read' the pictures in books. Reading a book is one way to make sure you're both looking at the same thing. At this stage, babies still won't follow a story, but by ten to twelve months of age they'll be able to focus on pictures. Big, clear, simple pictures of everyday objects are best at first. Many books have clever, quirky pictures that appeal to parents, but they're not ideal for very small children who prefer pictures of what they know.

When small children are ready to move on to more complex books, they'll still be much more interested in the pictures than the words. So rather than reading what the words say, it's good to 'read' the pictures – talk about them, even without telling a story at all.

Let your baby hold the book and turn the pages. Somewhere around this age children start wanting to turn the pages – in fact, turning pages is usually much more fascinating than listening to stories or even looking at pictures. Cardboard books or small cloth books where the pages don't tear can be useful, though a determined one-year-old can demolish even cardboard books rather quickly. Perhaps keep some books with your baby's toys. Even babies will enjoy 'reading' a book by themselves if they can crawl to it and pick it up.

⚛ WHAT DOES SCIENCE TELL US?

The importance of cuddles and chatting

Many young children were raised in orphanages in Romania in the 1980s. They had almost no early interaction with adults and received little affection or language stimulation. They were only changed and fed. Researchers found that these children, especially those not adopted by age two, showed less brain activity and very strange behaviours when they were older. These sad findings highlight the value of your early interaction with your baby – even when they're not yet talking back to you.

Summary of tips

- Imitate your baby.
- Ask them to do simple things.
- Sing to them.
- Talk about what they're looking at.
- 'Read' the pictures in books.
- Let your baby hold the book and turn the pages.

6.

Eureka! First words

Twelve months to eighteen months

It's said that it takes 10,000 hours of practice to master a skill such as playing a musical instrument or a top-level sport. The motor skills necessary are learnt with repeated practice – starting with early hit-and-miss efforts and gradually gaining more control and success. Nobody has estimated how much time a baby puts in when practising sounds and learning to talk, but what is certain is that they start in a very hit-and-miss way and gradually become as skilled as everyone around them.

Somewhere around twelve months of age babies usually start to walk and they also reach that magic language milestone: saying their first words. And just as some babies start to walk much earlier or much later than others, but they still learn to walk normally, so some babies start to talk earlier and some later but they still learn to talk.

Language and motor skills

One thing becomes obvious at around twelve months: your child probably won't progress at the same rate in both motor skills and in speech. Most small children seem to have a burst either in motor skills – such as walking, climbing, jumping – or in language. If they're more skilled in motor development they

often have relatively few words, and if they're more skilled in language they often don't run around as much. Small children do seem to concentrate on one area or the other at a time.

First words

It's not always easy to pick those magic first words. Sometimes they're obvious, because the first word is very different from the sounds the baby is using when babbling. And sometimes the first words sound just like that babble.

What is perhaps surprising is that there seems to be no way to predict what your baby's first word will be. It seems to depend entirely on what interests them and what is in their environment. For one small boy who adored the family's cats, 'cat' was an expected word. 'Up' is another common first word, with or without arms raised to be picked up, or said defiantly as the baby crawls or climbs up the stairs. 'Railway-line' isn't an expected first word, but it was the first recognisable word a train-mad small boy said.

Babble or words

One child's favourite babble sound was 'da'. When she met her grandmother's cocker spaniel for the first time, she pointed at it with delight and said 'da!' It certainly wasn't very distinctive. In fact, her mother thought Nanna was over-interpreting when she insisted that her granddaughter had just said 'dog'.

That night at bedtime, the baby and her mother followed their usual routine of playing a music box. As the mother started the music box, the baby said 'music box' very clearly – not the most common first word, but most definitely a true word!

What sorts of words will they say?

First words aren't always the names of things. Sometimes 'mum' and 'dad' continue on from a baby's babble and become true words, but 'that', 'wassat' (what's that said as one word), 'down' or 'there' are just as common as names. And although you can't easily predict the first words a baby will say, by the time they've learnt about fifty words you can predict the sorts of words they're likely to have. We'll talk about this in more detail in Chapter 8, but for now it's worth noting that people's names, words for animals like 'dog' or 'cat', foods like 'nana' or 'bickie' and body parts such as 'nose' are common early words.

Moving from babble to words

Just as babies produce very different first words, so they don't
all move from babble to words in the same way. There seem to
be two main routes that babies follow as they move from babble
into words. Some babies keep babbling and then, all at once, you
realise that there are a few real words mixed in with the babble
– but it's often very hard to spot the real words, when so much
is babble. Other babies stop babbling and have a quiet period –
sometimes as long as a month – without saying much, and then
start to use real words. It's much easier to spot their first real
words because they're not buried in the middle of lots of babble.

Strings of nonsense sounds

Just because your child can now say a few words it doesn't mean
that these are all they will use when they talk. Everyone around
them is talking fluently, and that's what they want to do too. So
somewhere around the same time as they start to use words, they
also start to make long strings of nonsense sounds. It sounds like
language, with rhythm and pitch patterns, but often there aren't
any real words used. But your child will demand your attention
and expect a response. They may even pull your head around so
you know they're talking to you. The pitch patterns mark some
of these utterances clearly as questions to which your small
child wants an answer. This can be somewhat complicated: how
can you answer them when you have no idea at all what they're
saying? Parents usually manage to work out ways of providing
answers, with the time honoured 'you show me' often working
very well. It must be very frustrating for a young child to ask a
question and not get a sensible answer.

> ### 🔬 Wʜᴀᴛ ᴅᴏᴇs sᴄɪᴇɴᴄᴇ ᴛᴇʟʟ us?
>
> **Quantity counts**
>
> Hearing 'a lot of language' is positively related to children producing 'a lot of language'. This was a key finding of a study that confirmed how important parents are in their children's language learning. The study also found that parents often use helpful strategies, such as using gestures alongside their speech to assist their child's understanding.

How much are they saying?

It's very easy to underestimate how much a baby or toddler is saying. When someone says to us, 'My fifteen-month-old isn't saying anything – is he okay?' the first thing we do is mentally change 'anything' to 'much' because most babies, especially first children, say more than their parents recognise. And then we ask 'Is he really active? Running around and climbing?' and if the answer is, 'Oh yes, he's always been very active' then we usually suggest that he's probably going through a motor development phase. The words will soon come – keep your ears open. It really does seem that young children can't do two things at once. They seem to have a burst of doing motor things, and then a burst of words. But do make sure you keep talking to them in simple sentences, and if you are worried talk to a health professional or preschool teacher about it.

More to say: ideas for parents ♀

- **Repeat what they say.** Once your baby has some words, it's very important that you reinforce them. When your one-year-old comes over with their arms up and says 'up', it's very easy to just pick them up and carry on with what you're doing. But it's really good to say, 'Up you come' or something like that as you pick them up.

- **Put their word into a simple sentence.** It's helpful to put their word into a sentence – but keep it simple! If they say 'bickie' you can say, 'You want a bickie? Let's find a bickie. Bickie for Adam.' It's good if you can make their word the start or the end of the sentence, as these are the parts that babies seem to notice most. At first, the words in the middle of a sentence seem to be ignored.

- **One or two words is enough,** especially if your child isn't saying too much yet. For example, when they're playing with blocks in a container you can say, 'block out, block out … block in, block in' and if you'd rather use a more complete sentence then perhaps say, 'block's out, block's out … block's in, block's in'. But don't make it more complex – 'the block's out' is probably too much, and 'you're taking the block out' is way too much at this stage.

- **Comment, comment, comment.** As before, it's good to keep commenting on everything that's happening – but make sure that what you're talking about is happening right now, and preferably that your baby is looking at the same thing you are. It's not very helpful if you're talking about the cat on the chair while the baby is looking out the window at a dog on the street.

- **Encourage repetitive activities.** Somewhere during this period your baby will usually start to focus on some motor activity and do it over and over again. They'll take every toy out of a box and then put them all back in. Or, if you let them, they'll empty everything out of the kitchen cupboards or drawers and probably put them back in different places … Once your baby starts to do this sort of thing your language opportunities increase apace. You can comment on what they're taking out – 'block, block, 'nother block, block' as they empty the block container, and then 'all gone' when it's empty. Or you can say, 'out, out, out' as they come out and 'in, in, in' as they go back in.

- **Comment on what they're doing as they're doing it.** It's particularly helpful if you comment on what your baby is doing as they're doing it. This reinforces the tie between language and the world.

- **Avoid colours.** At this early stage, avoid colours. This is very hard for us to do since we almost automatically comment on colour – 'car, that's a red car'. But colours are particularly hard for small children. Most three-year-old children only really know two colours, so when your baby is just starting to use words, give colours a miss. (We'll talk more about colours in Chapter 18.)

- **You don't need to 'teach' them.** It's great to think about ways to stimulate your child's language and learning but you don't need to actually *teach* young children. One of the wonders of language learning is that your child will learn language without you consciously teaching it. As you talk to them about what's going on around them, so they learn language.

- **Keep it simple.** At this stage, when you're commenting to your child on what they're doing, a good rule is 'two ideas per sentence' – 'Mummy is hanging the washing. Hanging the shirt. Hanging the socks. Hanging the towels' – assuming that they're outside with you. It's usually better to avoid, 'Mummy's hanging the shirt' because the word in the middle – hanging – is often just not heard. And since words like hanging that go in the middle of sentences are usually verbs and verbs are essential for language development, it's good to make them stand out at the start of your sentence rather than burying them in the middle.

📖 Talking and reading times

Simple picture books are ideal at this stage, especially books with pictures of things your child will recognise. When your child looks at a picture they have to translate the flat, two-dimensional images into the three dimensions of the real objects. This is much harder than it seems. And when they start to play with toys, they have to learn to associate small toys like cars and dolls with real objects that are often much larger.

Point out pictures of your child's early words. When you're reading a book, emphasise the words your child knows such as their favourite foods – (ba)nana; body parts – eyes, toes; and animals – cat, dog, cow, duck.

Look for things in the pictures. Children at this age probably still don't want to listen to the words of a book unless there's a lot of repetitive language in the book, such as in *The Very Hungry Caterpillar* by Eric Carle. They'd rather hunt for something small in a picture. Books where there's a bird or a snail or something similar hidden on every page are ideal. And you can talk about the picture – 'Look at the truck. We saw a truck. Remember? We were going to the shops. The truck drove past. It made a lot of noise.' Eventually the child will say their version of 'truck!' as they look at the picture.

> ### 💬 Talking point
>
> Your baby makes a long string of nonsense babble sounds.
>
> You might say, 'Oh, you do have a lot to say! What do you want to tell me?'
>
> Your baby says 'Car!'
>
> You might say 'That's Nanna's car. Nanna's here.'

Summary of tips

- Repeat what they say.
- Put their word into a simple sentence.
- One or two words is enough.
- Comment, comment, comment.
- Encourage repetitive activities.
- Comment on what they're doing as they're doing it.
- Avoid colours.
- You don't need to 'teach' them.
- Keep it simple.
- Simple picture books are ideal at this stage.
- Point out pictures of your child's early words.
- Look for things in the pictures.

7.

Thinking, play and language

Birth to three-plus years

Ten-month-old Sara picks up a long block and puts it to her ear as if it's a mobile phone.

Her slightly older friend Jemma pulls a box over to the table and stands on it to get a sipper cup near the edge (fortunately her mother's coffee cup is too far away).

Twenty-month-old Lachlan watches the hammer throw at the local sports ground and then enthusiastically twirls his toy golf club. He is about to let it fly when his mother saves the situation.

These children have obviously learnt some motor skills, but that's not all they've learnt.

Motor skills and language

A lot has to happen before a baby is able to use words. Many important pre-language skills don't seem to have much to do with language. For language to develop, children need to be able to use a toy such as a block to represent something else. This is what Sara did when she pretended the block was a phone. They also need to be able to use 'tools' – such as dragging a stool over to the table to reach a biscuit. This is what Jemma did when she pulled the box to the table to get the sipper cup. And they also need to be able to remember so they can delay before they copy someone else's behaviour. This is what Lachlan did when he was about to use his toy golf club like a throwing hammer.

It takes a while before children are able to remember what someone did and then do it themselves much later. Unfortunately for his parents, Jake remembered very early how to turn an iPad on and off – and delighted in doing so when his parents were trying to send emails.

Piaget, permanence and play

Many of our ideas about how children think and learn have been shaped by Swiss psychologist, Jean Piaget. Piaget observed children's behaviour and described cognitive development from birth to adolescence.

Grasping to repetitive play

Children up to eighteen to 24 months of age learn about their world mainly through their senses and motor behaviours. This starts with reflex movements such as grasping and sucking. Over time, goal-directed behaviour emerges. Early goal-directed behaviour includes emptying all the blocks out of a box, putting them back and then doing it all over again.

The magic of disappearance

By around eight to twelve months children come to understand that something still exists when they can no longer see it – this is known as object permanence. Think of a child's response to a game of peek-a-boo. A very young child reacts with surprise and then delight when your face emerges from behind a cloth. An older child pulls the cloth away because they know your face is hidden behind it.

Language on the horizon

We take it for granted that a picture or a sound can represent an object. But as we noted, this ability to understand symbols is something that children have to learn. Piaget initially described this understanding as occurring from about two years, but some people consider it begins to develop at a very early age, even before one.

Piaget believed that before a child could develop language, they had to use representational or make-believe play, use tools, and be able to defer or delay imitating someone.

✕ WHAT DOES SCIENCE TELL US?

Sharing the fun

Children's experiences at home are critical to early language and learning. According to research, having a responsive parent, sharing activities such as regular book reading, and having age-appropriate toys and books make all the difference,

The importance of play

Play is children's work – and they really do work hard at it. But at first your baby won't play with anyone else; they'll play in the same room as another small child (for a short time), but they won't actually do anything with the other child. Soon, however, they'll both play side by side. They'll want to play with similar toys – or try to grab each other's toys. They're still not exactly playing *with* each other, but now they're at least playing beside each other. They'll probably talk to their own toys, imitate each other or just talk to themselves. But even though both children are doing similar things, they probably won't talk to each other as they play.

Eventually, they'll start to play cooperatively. They'll start to share the toys and your child will actually start to talk to the other child. This sometimes doesn't happen until they're about four years old, so don't worry if your three-year-old still wants all the toys for themselves.

✖️ WHAT DOES SCIENCE TELL US?

Talking books

Interactive book reading has been shown to improve children's language. In one study, the parent or teacher talked about the book they were reading and also ensured that the child could play with concrete objects that were represented in the book so they learnt the words in meaningful contexts. The children who were engaged in interactive book reading had larger vocabularies and better language skills than children who passively listened as books were read to them.

Table 2: **Movement and play milestones**

	Movement and physical development	Play
Birth to 3 months	• Turns to sound. • Looks at things. • Grasps at things.	• Plays with their hands. • Focuses on a simple, bright mobile. • Grasps at things. • Can't yet bring something in front of their face and look at it.
3 to 6 months	• Grasps things. • Mouths things. • Interacts with you.	• Rattles that they can hold easily are good. • They'll probably enjoy a mobile to lie under, hung over their cot or pram, and will swing at it with their hands. • Your baby will focus on your face and 'talk' to you.
6 months to 9 months	• Sits up. • Interacts with you. • Still mouths things. • Tries to get things that are out of reach. • May begin to rock back and forth or crawl backwards.	• Will bring something to their face so they can look at it. • Everything will go into their mouth – this is the main way they explore things at present. • Starts to enjoy exploring noisy toys and may be able to push a large button that makes a sound. • Simple colourful toys they can pick up and put down can be good e.g. nesting cups. • Will enjoy simple bath toys with you. • Will enjoy movement e.g. rocking in your arms, in a bouncer or on a baby swing; these are all great opportunities for talking to them, for saying rhymes, playing finger games and singing songs.
9 months to 12 months	• Sits up. • Becoming mobile. • Rolls over. • Crawling. • Pulls up on furniture. • Stands alone.	• Soon your baby will realise that 'out of sight' isn't 'out of mind', that things are still there even when they can't see them. If you have a pet, your baby may start to look for it when it isn't in the room. If they've started to move around round – crawling, rolling – they'll start to move towards toys. If they're only moving backwards, they may get frustrated when they can't reach a toy they want. • An activity centre will come into its own now. It doesn't have to be expensive. They'll love to shake a container with a very secure lid and noisy things inside it. Or bang two blocks together or hit a pot with a spoon! • Your baby will probably enjoy putting things into a container and tipping them out again. A simple shape sorter is good, and if it's too hard take off the lid and your baby will enjoy just putting the shapes in.

Table 2: **Movement and play milestones continued**

12 months to 18 months	• Walks. • Hand control. • Plays next to another child.	• Your baby will start to build towers with blocks – they probably won't be able to balance more than three or four blocks on top of each other, and the greatest fun is knocking them down. • They will start to enjoy pretend play – a large cardboard box can be a car or a train or a boat. • Your baby will love water play, which is best outside on a warm day or in the bath. • Toys still go into their mouth, so you still need big toys, and toys with parts that won't break off.
18 months to 2 years	• Walks alone and may walk up steps. • Can pull a toy while walking or begin to push themselves on a ride-on toy. • Can help undress themselves. • Can drink from a cup and eat with a spoon.	• Now your child is mobile, they'll enjoy outdoor play. They may enjoy going to the park and playing on the swings, and perhaps on the slide. You'll have to go down the slide with them, or put them on part way up and hold them as they slide down. • Knows what ordinary things are for and enjoys playing with them e.g. holding a phone to their ear, combing their hair or their teddy's hair. • Begins to scribble on paper – check that those crayons are put away afterwards!
2 years to 3 years	• Kicks a ball. • Runs freely. • Walks up and down stairs holding on. • Climbs onto furniture unaided. • Throws ball overhand. • May use one hand more than the other. • Builds towers of four or more blocks. • Copies straight lines and circles.	• Will mainly play beside other children and need encouragement to share toys. • Begins to include other children in simple games such as chasing. • Plays simple make-believe games. Begins to act out in play things they have observed in their daily life e.g. if they have a younger brother or sister, they may start to feed, bathe and change their toys or pretend to do household chores. • Enjoys physical play that allows them to practise the motor skills they are learning. Will enjoy rolling a ball to someone else. Kicking, throwing and catching balls with someone can still be frustrating for most children as many go in the wrong direction or are missed. 'Balloon tennis' – patting a balloon to someone else – is easier and makes a good inside game for a very active child.

Table 2: **Movement and play milestones continued**

Beyond 3 years		
	• Runs easily. • Pedals a tricycle. • Climbs easily. • Can turn door handles, unscrew jars and work toys with moving parts, buttons and levers.	• Plays make-believe games with toy dolls/people, animals, cars etc. • Can complete simple puzzles with three or four pieces. • From about 4 years, plays with other children and may begin to enjoy simple card and board games with older children or adults – the easiest card games are snap or matching games. Board games like snakes and ladders can be played once your child can count to six – but you may have to choose when the game ends rather than play it to the finish! • Play begins to reflect the particular interests of the child – some children love to use blocks and Lego, some like very active play, some like to colour and draw … but it is important that your child does lots of different things in play so all aspects of their development are encouraged.

💬 Talking point

You are reading a book with your baby. They point to a picture of a ball and say 'ball'.

You might say, 'That's a ball. You've got a ball like that. You like your ball. We took it to the park.'

More to say: ideas for parents ♀

- **Safety comes first for toys and other playthings.** At all ages, safety has to be the first consideration when it comes to play. All young children tend to put things in their mouths as part of exploring them. This is why good toys for very young children need to be bigger (so they can't be swallowed) and are sturdy so that bits can't break off (and again, be swallowed). As your child gets older and you notice they are no longer 'mouthing' toys, you can pick smaller toys for them to use in play.

- **You lead the play.** When your child is very young, play happens when they're interacting with you and other family members. Their play happens as you hold them on your knee or as you're carrying them on your shoulder.

Rhymes

You can use rhymes and songs like *Rock-a-bye Baby* or *My Hands are Clapping Just Like Yours* to play with your baby.

Rock-a-bye baby on the treetop. When the wind blows the cradle will rock. When the bough breaks, the cradle will fall. And down will come baby, cradle and all.

Sing this with your baby sitting on your knee facing you, and hold them firmly under the armpits. Rock from side to side as you sing. Lean them back gently for 'fall' and pause very briefly, and then bring them back upright. Then do it all again.

- **Give them lots of different play experiences.** Repetition is an important part of learning and children may do the same thing over and over when they are very young. Your child will have favourite toys and games at all ages, but extend them with something new and different to try. Think of some of the things you enjoyed when you were little or that you've seen other children of a similar age enjoy.

- **Play alongside your child.** Before your child can play *with* you, it's really helpful if you play alongside them. Copy what they're doing and comment on it as you do so. At first they may not talk to you or actually play *with* you, but eventually you'll be able to play together.

- **Comment rather than asking questions.** It's tempting to ask your small child what they're doing or what they've made when they're busy playing by themselves beside you. But it's much better to comment on what you're doing, or on what they're doing, than to ask questions. Especially if your child seems a bit reluctant to talk, questions can just make them even more silent whereas, one day, they'll suddenly respond to one of your comments.

📖 Talking and reading times

Read and recite nursery rhymes. There is a huge range of brightly illustrated books containing individual nursery rhymes *(One, Two, Where is my Shoe?)* or collections of common ones, such as the Ladybird collection of 21 rhymes including: *Humpty Dumpty, Mary Had a Little Lamb, Sing a Song of Sixpence* and many more. What were some of your favourites as a child? Children will love to hear you read these, or read and say them with you, from when they are a baby right up to the age of about three-and-a-half.

Books about their experiences and play will be enjoyed. Your child will love to see a book about the things they are doing and seeing – in life and in play. For a one- to two-year-old child, this might be books about everyday activities such as the *Maisy* series by Lucy Cousins (*Maisy's Bathtime, Maisy's Bedtime*, etc.). From about age three your child will love to see books about things they are interested in; *The Little Yellow Digger* series of books by Betty and Alan Gilderdale, for example, are very popular with children interested in construction sites, building with blocks or playing with toy vehicles.

Choose short picture books to start. Pick very short picture book stories for your younger child and gradually build up to longer ones as their attention and memory skills increase with age.

Play a naming game. Your child will be able to point out common things in picture books from about two years. Let them find the bird in the picture, for example.

Give your child the opportunity to make sounds and finish sentences. Young children enjoy simple story books that give them a chance to participate by imitating sounds of animals or making vehicle noises as you read the story together. As they get a bit older, your child will be able to finish a sentence or rhyme or 'read' (say) the words coming up on the next page in a familiar book.

Have books where your child can reach them and 'read' them. Choose small books your child can hold. Keep some little books in the car for them to read in their car seat. Keep other lager books for bedtime reading together.

Summary of tips

- Safety comes first for toys and other playthings.
- You lead the play.
- Give them lots of different play experiences.
- Play alongside your child.
- Comment rather than asking questions.
- Read and recite nursery rhymes.
- Books about their experiences and play will be enjoyed.
- Choose short picture books to start.
- Play a naming game.
- Give your child the opportunity to make sounds and finish sentences.
- Have books where your child can reach them and 'read' them.

8.

The one-word stage: expanding words and worlds

Nine months to 24 months

Fifty is a magic number when your child is learning their first words. There's no way you can predict what your baby's first word will be, or their second word, for that matter. But we can predict that by the time your baby can say around fifty words their language development will be well underway. They'll be able to talk about lots of different things and express many different types of meaning. Fifty really is a magic number.

What will they talk about?

Your child will probably have one or more words for *animals* – perhaps 'cat' or 'dog'. Lots of children also say 'duck' because they feed the ducks in the park and play with ducks in the bath. They'll probably also have words for *people* – something for 'mummy' and 'daddy', though what they say will depend on what you say, and also some way to refer to themselves, either a version of their name or else 'baby'. They'll have words for *toys* like 'block' or 'ball' and *vehicles* like 'car' or 'truck' or 'bus' and *clothing*, especially things that can be taken off easily like 'hat' or 'shoe' or 'sock'. *Household items* like 'clock' or 'light' are common as are *foods*, especially '(ba)nana' or 'milk' and *things to eat or drink with* like 'bottle' or 'cup'. They'll usually have a *descriptive word* or two, with the first often being 'hot' (you have to use it so often for safety reasons) or 'pretty'. And finally, words for *greeting* – 'hi' and 'bye'. And by now 'bye' has become a true word that doesn't have to have the action with it (though often it still does).

Early types of meaning

Animals – cat or dog
People – mummy, daddy, baby
Toys – block or ball
Vehicles – car or truck or bus
Clothing - hat or shoe or sock
Household items – clock or light
Foods – (ba)nana or milk
Things to eat or drink with – bottle or cup
Descriptive words – hot or pretty
Greetings – hi and bye

Patterns in language

At first your child will learn one word at a time, and each word will be a totally separate item. But by the time they can use about fifty words they'll start to see patterns in the ways words are pronounced. Fiona picked up her dad's mobile phone and said 'phone'. It was clear and everyone knew what she meant. But a week or two later, they wondered what the word 'doe' meant – Fiona had dropped the end of 'phone' and changed the 'f' sound to 'd' so it was easier for her to say. Eventually her family worked it out, but children's early pronunciations often take a lot of detective work. We'll look more at pronunciation in Chapters 13 and 14.

An increase in 'errors' means progress

This is the first example of something that happens over and over again as children learn language: an increase in 'errors' means progress. At first this seems crazy – how can it be good if they're making mistakes? But as your child learns more language, there are many more places where they can make 'errors'. These errors show that they're experimenting with what they're learning, and that's good.

The 'vocabulary explosion'

Your child's first 50 words often seem to come painfully slowly, one at a time. And to the confusion of parents, they're often said only once and then never again so you start to wonder if you imagined hearing them. But once your child reaches that magic 50-word mark, new words seem to appear in spurts. What is often called a vocabulary explosion can occur and you lose track of just how many words your child can say.

✖ WHAT DOES SCIENCE TELL US?

Another day another two to five words

Research has shown that most eighteen-month-olds learn an average of two to five new words a day. The researchers say this highlights how important it is to talk a lot to young children and label everything in their environment. For example, name the food your child is eating and the things they see when you go out together.

Giant words

Once children are using single words, it often sounds as though they progress very quickly onto two words together. 'Look at', 'wassat' or 'gimme' are phrases that sound like two words, but if you listen carefully you won't hear your child say 'look' or 'what' though they may well say 'that'. Most children learn these combinations as wholes – known as 'giant words' – and they can't yet use the two words separately.

One word at a time

Some children use chains of single words to say what they want. 'Drink. [Pause] Nate.' Or 'Cat. [Pause] Gone. [Pause] There.' Soon these chains of words will become two- or three-word 'sentences' but at first it seems as though your child can only say one word at a time. It's clear they're not joined into 'sentences' because each word has its own clear pitch pattern, and sounds complete. But eventually 'Drink, Nate' will sound like a proper two-word 'sentence'.

⬚ Talking point

Your baby says, 'Dog. Bark.'

You might say, 'Yes, that dog *is* barking. He's making a noise. Lots of noise.'

More to say: ideas for parents ⬚

- **Carry on commenting.** Again, the most important thing is to keep talking. Comment on what you're doing or, even better, on what your child is doing. And keep what you say short – 'there's a car, on the road, going along the road. Oh, all gone.' The precise words don't matter, so long as your child is paying attention.

- **Be alert for the 'errors' that show progress.** Another important thing you can do at the one-word stage is to be alert for examples of the 'errors' that actually mean progress. It's important to know about this because others – often grandparents and neighbours – can be concerned when children aren't as easy to understand as they used to be. You can reassure them (and yourself) that nothing is wrong and your child is just making things easier for themselves as they learn.

● **Don't imitate your child's cute pronunciations.** Children's early pronunciations are often very cute – the 'dider' who goes 'der' is clearly a tiger who goes 'grrr'. It can be very tempting for the rest of the family – especially older brothers and sisters – to start calling tigers 'diders', but it's not helpful for the child who genuinely thinks they're saying 'tiger' just like everyone else.

● **Comprehension comes first.** So far your child is only saying one word at a time, and not many of them, but they'll be understanding many more. So you can ask children who are at the one-word stage to do lots of things – such as 'Go and get your slippers' or 'Where is my glasses case?' (when you know they've gone and hidden it again). If you do this often enough, the slippers will usually be brought to you, but the child may have genuinely forgotten where they hid your glasses case.

● **Don't ask them to perform!** It's tempting to try to get your child to show off their new language skills. Parents often ask 'What's that?' expecting the child to say 'light' or 'cat' or some other word they know. Some children oblige and enjoy this, but many children don't. Unless your child is actively looking at or playing with something, they often won't say its name – which can be very frustrating for a proud parent. And when they do use their new words they often fly past so fast that you miss them. Don't worry, soon they'll talk so much you'll wish they'd stop.

📖 Talking and reading times

Let them 'read' books by themselves. By now your child may want to 'read' books by themselves and may especially want to turn the pages. At this age they'll probably get bored before you reach the end of a book, or they may want to read the book upside down. That's okay; they're still getting used to books and what to do with them.

Repetition – read it again! Your child will probably want you to read their favourite book over and over again until the book 'accidentally' gets lost. They'll like repetitive stories or songs, and will repeat 'e-i-e-i-o' – or their version of it – for *Old Macdonald had a farm* and fill in words in favourite books.

Sometimes the pictures tell the story rather than the words. By now, your child will enjoy it when you read them shorter stories, but they probably still won't want to listen to longer or more complicated ones. For some children, it may still be better to 'read' the story from the pictures rather than reading all the words.

Ask questions and follow up on what they say. Ask simple questions about what you can both see in the book. When your child answers, follow up with another question or a comment.

Follow their interests. You don't need to talk about every page or every picture. If your child is particularly interested in parts of the book, focus on those and enjoy looking at them/reading them together.

Keep them interested in the book. The longer you and your child can spend reading a book, the better. You can extend the reading time by hunting for things in the pictures. Your child will enjoy finding the baby in the picture, for example, or the cat or dog, especially if what they're looking for is partly hidden. And focusing on the details of a picture is a good way to get them used to concentrating on a book. But don't go over the top – you've both got to enjoy it!

Summary of tips

- Carry on commenting.
- Be alert for the 'errors' that show progress.
- Don't imitate your child's cute pronunciations.
- Comprehension comes first.
- Don't ask them to perform!
- Let them 'read' books by themselves.
- Repetition – read it again!
- Sometimes the pictures tell the story rather than the words.
- Ask questions and follow up on what they say.
- Follow their interests.
- Keep them interested in the book.

9.

What's the use of language, anyway?

Nine months to 24 months

How will your baby get from crying to interactive play? And will they bother? By the time they're one year old, babies can make themselves understood amazingly well even without any 'proper' language – so why bother with learning words? Already they can show when they're hungry, when they've had enough to eat, when they want to play with something and when they're tired. What can they do with words that they can't do without them? And how many words do they need – is one word at a time enough?

What can a child do with just one word?

You'll be spending lots of time watching your baby and seeing what they can do. The linguist M.A.K. Halliday also spent a lot of time watching his son, Nigel. He was amazed to discover that even though Nigel could only use one word at a time, he could use his words to do seven different sorts of things. Halliday called these *language functions.* You might think that Nigel had a special advantage because his father was a linguist. But we've discovered that almost all small children use language in similar ways, even when they can only use one word at a time.

I want something!

The simplest of the functions is the *instrumental* function – your child uses it when they want something. They may say 'bottle' or '(ba)nana' when they're hungry or 'hat' when they want to go outside and know that putting on their hat is part of the routine. Using words means that babies can control many more things and get more of what they want. You'll already be very good at working out what your baby wants even though they're not using words; but when words are added, it's just so much easier for everyone.

Do something!

The next function is the *regulatory* function – used to get other people to do what you want. Babies usually 'organise' their parents, and sometimes they organise older brothers or sisters as well. 'Up' or 'down' are typical early words that can be used to give orders. And parents often hurry to do what small children want – something that can frustrate older children who don't get nearly as prompt service.

Let's do something together!

Sometimes one-year-olds want you to do something for them – feed them or cuddle them, for example. Other times they want you to play with them. When you realise your child wants to play with you, they're using the *interactional* function. Peek-a-boo or games of clapping are typical, and even if they start without words the appropriate words are soon added. At first you'll have to start these games with your baby, but after a while your baby will start them. Sam used to hide behind the side of his car seat and then peek out with laughter whenever someone was sitting next to him in the car. Sam would always start the game and his 'playmate' usually tired of it long before he did.

Lots of language can be added in a game of peek-a-boo and you can add lots of exaggerated facial expressions and intonation: 'Where's Sam? Sam's gone. There he is, hello Sam! Oh, Sam's gone again. I wonder where Sam is? Oh, there he is!'

I like this!

Small children are interested in everything that's going on around them. When they comment on what they're noticing, that's using the *personal* function. 'Cat' as your one-year-old strokes the long-suffering family cat, or chases it madly across the room, expresses what interests them at that moment. And words for food (like 'nana') or for toys (like 'block') similarly express the personal function, as that's what they're currently focused on.

You can usually work out what your child means when they use the earlier functions – instrumental, regulatory or interactional – because context helps. But when they start to use words to comment on what they're interested in right now (the personal function), it gets harder. Unless you happen to be focusing on them and actually notice what they're looking at, it's all too easy to misunderstand.

Jake was fascinated by cars and ran across the room to look out the window every time he heard one coming up the street. So it was not surprising when he spent one afternoon pointing to his toy car and his parents' car in the drive and saying 'tar'. When he pointed at the fence and said 'tar' his grandmother was about to say, 'No, that's the fence' when she realised he was actually pointing to the car parked across the road. A conversation saved at the very last minute.

Let's explore!

Children are curious. They love to explore. When your child explores, they're using the *heuristic* function. *Heuristic* means learning by experience and that's what your child is doing all the time. Older children are always asking 'Why?' But even one-year-olds use language to explore. They'll say 'That?' or 'Wassat?' when they want to know what something is. And to your surprise, they'll often say 'Wassat?' and point to something when you know they already know its name. 'Wassat?' has become a game and your child seems to need you to ask 'What's that?' back to them so they can triumphantly give you the answer. You can find out more about 'Wassat?' and other 'terrible questions' in Chapter 16.

Let's pretend!

When they're about a year old, many children 'talk' to themselves as they go to sleep and when they wake up. At first it's just babble, but once your baby has some words you may hear them practising in their cot. Older children play with new sentences in the same way: 'Car, cars, two cars, lots of cars, truck, big truck …' And other children play with sounds making all sorts of nonsense words. One child had a brother called Simon, and he talked himself to sleep saying 'Simon, Nimon, Piemon, Lymon, Simon …' Fortunately his younger brother wasn't old enough to get upset at the mess he was making of his name. This is the *imaginative* function of language – playing with language for its own sake. Not all children use this function, but when they do use it, and you notice them, it's fun, so enjoy it!

Let me tell you …

Your one-year-old will often come and tell you things, but they are usually things you already know. You know much more than they do, so it's not often they can use the *informative* function and tell you something really new. It's not surprising that this is the last function to appear, and that some parents don't actually notice their child using it at all. But many children do use it even when they can only use one word at a time.

When John was fifteen months old he came to his mother in the kitchen and said 'gone'. His mother asked what had gone, and just got the response 'gone'. And then, even more strongly 'allgone'. So she followed the time-honoured practice of parents everywhere and said 'show me', only to be led to the toilet. And the toilet paper was indeed 'gone' and the toilet was filled with a soggy mess. That was definitely the informative function.

Table 3: Early functions of language

What they say The simpler language functions are above the double line.	What it means	Function
'Nana!' (I want a banana)	I want something!	Instrumental
'Up!' (Pick me up)	Do something!	Regulatory
'Peek-a-boo!'	Let's do something together!	Interactional
'Cat!' (Look, there's the cat!)	I like this!	Personal
'Wassat?' (But the child often wants to give the answer themselves at this stage)	Let's explore!	Heuristic
Rhyming language	Let's pretend!	Imaginative
'Gone.' (I've put all the paper into the toilet)	Let me tell you …	Informative

🔬 WHAT DOES SCIENCE TELL US?

Quiet babies need chatty parents

Parents don't always realise how important it is to talk to babies who can't yet talk. If a baby doesn't cry much and is happy spending lots of time alone in their cot, they sometimes get less one-on-one time with their parent or caregiver. This can also happen to toddlers who can't easily be understood. Researchers believe hearing less language in the home might explain some of the differences in children's early language learning.

Saying several things at once

Because small children can only use one word at a time, they can only express one function at a time. We all still use these basic language functions but we combine them in sophisticated ways. If you say something like, 'Why don't you make a cup of coffee, then we can watch that movie on TV,' you're combining into one sentence the instrumental function ('I want a cup of coffee'), regulatory function ('you get the coffee') and the interactional function ('we'll watch the movie together').

Your baby will soon be able to combine several functions in the same utterance. Once they can put words and functions together into 'sentences', they'll be able to interact in more complex ways.

By the time they're ready for school they can do so much

It's a busy afternoon at preschool. In the sandpit, five four-year-olds are earnestly going about the work of play.

Laura: I'm making a big hill for the cars to go up. Give me that digger, Jamie. Here's the bucket. You can get the water.

Jake: It's a lot of work ... Look at my hill.

Jamie: I'm a driver. I'm on the bulldozer. There's lots of buildings to pull down ... I'm making lots of roads.

Sam: We're very busy after the big storm ... I'm making roads too.

Jake: You can have this car, Nick ... I want the green one.

Stella: What are you making? I want to build a castle.

Laura: No, we've got to knock things down first, then we can build.

The five children playing in the sandpit have all learnt a lot about language. Although the activity and the sentences seem simple enough, they show just how much these children have learnt about language and interaction in their four years. There are informing statements, personal statements, requests, refusals and the start of interactive play.

These are all different ways of using language. Your baby can't use all of them yet, but you'll be surprised how many different things they can already do with their limited number of words.

More to say: ideas for parents ⚲

- **Notice what they're doing.** When your small child is working out what they can do with language, the most important thing for you to do is notice. If you're not aware of what they're doing or focusing on, you can easily misunderstand what they're trying to say. And when you add in the complexities of children's early pronunciations, the possibilities for misunderstanding increase greatly.

- **Let them take a turn at giving orders.** Some of the early language functions are used whenever you're both playing together. You'll use them as you ask your child for things and tell them to do something. And if you're willing to do what they ask you to, this lets them explore these early functions for themselves. And they don't even need words to play copycat. At ten months, Jeremy loved having people copy his actions – he'd put his hands up in the air and everyone was supposed to do the same. When they dutifully did, the look of delight on his face was wonderful. Even though he wasn't able to say words yet, he was practising the regulatory function by getting other people to do something, and the interactional function by doing the same thing together.

- **Share nursery rhymes in a game.** Nursery rhymes are wonderful for interaction. *Pat-a-cake, pat-a-cake baker's man ...*, or *Round and round the garden like a teddy bear ...*, need you both to be playing together. And both the rhyme and rhythm of nursery rhymes are also wonderful for the imaginative function, for the sheer joy of playing with language for its own sake.

📖 Talking and reading times

Read together. When your baby is at the one-word stage they're usually ready to 'read' simple books with you. Books with clear pictures of everyday objects are still best because they're still learning the skill of relating two-dimensional pictures to three-dimensional real world objects. At first, a book with a big colourful picture of one thing on a page is ideal. Once they're happy looking at a book with you, then more complex pictures are good. But they should still be pictures of the real world. A picture of a room lets you find chairs and tables and balls and blocks and lights and windows – all the things that are in the room around you.

Not too many words at first ... At the one-word stage, it's still more important to 'read' the pictures than the words. Except for nursery rhymes and books written with a really strong rhyme or rhythm, most early books have far too many words. At present, turning pages (one at a time if possible) and finding things in pictures is still the best way to 'read' to your young child. A book with good clear pictures, with the same object repeated somewhere in every picture, is still ideal. Your baby can learn to identify familiar things in the picture and you can both play 'hunt the teddy bear' or 'hunt the bird' in every picture.

💬 Talking point

Your child says, 'Digger. Me digger.'

You might say, 'Liam's got the digger. You take the bulldozer. You flatten the dirt that Liam digs out.'

Summary of tips

- Notice what they're doing.
- Let them take a turn at giving orders.
- Share nursery rhymes in a game.
- Read together.
- Not too many words at first …

10.

Early meanings:
look what I can tell you!

Nine months to 24 months

The sorts of things children can talk about expand rapidly between nine and 24 months. They may not use words exactly as you do, but they can get their meaning across very clearly.

Things move

Sasha is pushing a toy car round the room and saying, 'brmm-brmm'. Josh is pulling his circus train and bumping into blocks, 'choo-choo, choo-choo, there' (he says 'there' as the train hits another block). When we were at school, many of us learnt that action words are verbs. For Sasha and Josh, 'brmm-brmm' and 'choo-choo' are action words: they describe what the car and the train are doing. Later they'll learn more usual verbs like 'go' or 'bump' but at present, 'brmm-brmm' and 'choo-choo' work beautifully. Action is an important type of meaning to be able to express, and it doesn't matter which words your child first uses.

There!

Josh says 'there' as he bumps the train into a block. Hanna says 'there' as she completes a simple jigsaw. Sam says 'there' as he gives his mother two blocks. They're all talking about location, another useful early type of meaning. And although we usually think of 'here' and 'there' as a pair, your child will probably use 'there' long before 'here'. Some children, of course, use ''ere y'are' (here you are) as a 'giant word', but they don't usually use 'here' by itself.

As you can see from Josh, Hanna and Sam, early uses of 'there' can often almost mean, 'I've done it!' It's not long, however, before 'there' is used as a true location word. At first, though, it's only for places that are really close to your child, perhaps only places they can actually touch. It takes a while before a child can deal with distances that are further away from where *they* are.

🔬 Wнaт does science tell us?

Your response matters

Lots of interactive videos designed for babies and young children have characters who encourage the children to join in actions and activities. However, these videos aren't very successful by themselves in helping children learn new words. It's not the video format that's the problem – researchers found that two-year-olds could learn new words when interacting with a live person through Skype video calls. Instead back and forth social interaction seems to be the essential element. Researchers concluded that if we respond to children in a way that is meaningful to them they will learn – even via a screen. Similarly, children can learn from interactive videos so long as there's an adult to watch with them and talk about what they're seeing. But a face-to-face conversation is best of all.

Describing things

We all describe things – the sky is blue, the weather is warm or hot or freezing cold. A book is interesting or exciting or just plain boring. And children describe things too. Often the first describing word (or adjective), children use is 'hot'. Jake loves pointing to coffee cups (with screw-on lids for safety) and saying 'Cup. Hot.' He then very carefully touches the lid or the bottom (which is only just warm) and screws up his face. It's not surprising that 'hot' is often the first describing word that children use – we have to use it so often for safety! But another early describing word isn't concerned with safety. How often have you heard someone say to a small child, 'Look at the pretty flowers'? It's not surprising that children often pick up 'pretty' very early too. Another early describing word is 'big' – but not usually 'little'. Children usually comment on big things long before they talk about little things: big things are obviously much easier to notice.

The things they say!

Uncle Jim was playing cars with Nate.

> Uncle Jim: Let's put the cars in the big transporter.
> [Pause]
> Nate: I call the car carrier a 'car carrier'.
> Uncle Jim: Oh, okay. I'll call it a car carrier too.

Mine!

Possibly the most important word for a child with older brothers or sisters is 'mine'. Their brothers and sisters don't agree, of course, but younger children declare their own possessions at a very early age – and lay claim to things that don't belong to them as well. Yes, children need to learn to share but they have to be able to declare what is theirs as well. So possession is another important type of meaning. First children don't need to use 'mine' to declare their own things at home, and they may not use the meaning possession as early as second or later children do. But if they're playing with other children at preschool, then 'mine!' is really important for them too.

Things exist, disappear and reappear

Although the meanings we've talked about so far all seem simple enough to us as adults, they're actually surprisingly complicated. The very earliest meanings children use comment on things that are there in front of them, and that then disappear or reappear.

Out of sight out of mind

At first, children wonder whether things are still there when they can't see them. When they can no longer see something, then as far as they're concerned it no longer exists. This is wonderful when you want to hide car keys or precious things from your baby. They won't find things that are hidden even while they watch you hiding them.

But somewhere about nine months your baby will realise that out of sight isn't out of mind. And as soon as they know things continue to exist even when they can't see them (what Piaget called 'object permanence'), you have to be much more creative when you want to hide something. One family jokingly reckoned their baby son had iPad permanence long before he was aware that other objects were also permanent. He adored iPads (as did his parents), and from about eight months on it was impossible to hide them from him. He'd even pull at any cord he saw in the hope that an iPad would be attached …

No more cars

Ron is on his way to the shops. As he crosses the road he looks to the right, sees a car and waits. There are no more cars to the right, so he checks to the left – there's another car. He waits again. Finally there are no cars in either direction and he crosses.

His son Ollie is playing with cars on the table. 'Brrm-brrm,' he says as a car runs off the 'road' and onto the floor. Ollie grabs another car and says 'Brrm-brrm, more,' as the second car goes off the road and onto the floor. 'Gone,' says Ollie as he looks for another car. Then the two cars are rescued and the game starts again.

Ron and Ollie are both using the simplest of meaning types: **existence**, **recurrence** and **non-existence**. Both Ron and Ollie look for cars (existence) then look again (recurrence) and then check that there aren't any more (non-existence).

As soon as your baby achieves object permanence they'll realise that objects exist – and that it's possible for them not to exist. They'll also realise that things that disappear can reappear. The three categories of existence, recurrence and non-existence are the three most basic meaning categories in language – and in the world.

Early ways to express these categories of meaning are 'cat' or 'train' or whatever your baby really likes for existence; 'gone' or even just the name of an object (e.g. 'cat') and a shake of the head for non-existence/disappearance; and ''nother' or 'more' for recurrence.

Teddy come back

Louisa really loved a little book that had a teddy bear on every page except one. She'd read the book with her mother, saying 'Teddy, teddy' and pointing to the teddy until she came to the page where there wasn't a teddy. Then she'd say 'Teddy' in a very sad voice and shake her head, and on the next page she'd say 'Teddy' with a beaming smile. Although she was using the same word it was clear that Louisa was expressing existence, then sad non-existence and finally delighted recurrence.

Like Louisa, your child will learn these important meaning categories while they're playing with you and with others and learning about their environment.

Other forms of 'no'

We wouldn't get very far in life if we could only talk about things that exist, don't exist or recur. Non-existence is the earliest form of negative, often expressed as 'gone'. But very early on, small children also learn **rejection**. This is the most common negative and is expressed by 'no' said very firmly when your child doesn't want to do something (such as get dressed) or eat something, or even just exist. And 'no' can start well before the 'terrible twos'. 'No' isn't a word you'll rejoice at hearing, but it does show that your child is learning more about meaning.

There's another type of negative called **denial**. This is the hardest of the negatives and the last one your child will learn. But it's the one we tend to think of first when we think of negatives. We point to a picture of a dog and say 'That's a cat, isn't it?' and expect the child to say 'No, (it's a) dog'. And that really is asking a lot of a small child. In fact, it's way too hard for most small children!

Small children only need single words to express existence, recurrence, non-existence, rejection and denial, as well as the other early types of meaning we've talked about in this chapter. In fact it's amazing just how many different types of meaning they can express when they can only use one word at a time.

Animals don't usually tell lies

Denial is an incredibly important meaning category. One definition of what separates us humans from animals – and not a very flattering definition – is our ability to lie, and denial is essential for lying. We can tell lies, animals usually can't ...

In the United States, staff at the Gorilla Foundation taught sign language to Koko the gorilla. Koko asked for a kitten. It was given to her, and she looked after it tenderly. One day she tore a sink out of the wall of her house. When her handlers asked her who did it (using sign language) she signed back that the cat had caused the damage. Having the ability to communicate to humans allowed her to lie ...

Early types of meaning

Existence: 'car', 'dog', 'cat'
Recurrence: ''nother', 'more'
Non-existence/disappearance: 'gone', 'allgone'
Rejection: 'no'
Denial: 'no'

Other early types of meaning that only need one word

Action: 'brmm-brmm', 'up', 'choo-choo'
Location: 'there'
Description: 'hot', 'pretty'
Possession: 'mine!'

⬤ Talking point

Your child says, 'Gone.'
    You might say, 'Yes, the ball's gone. You threw it away.'

Your child touches your coffee cup and says, 'Hot!'
    You might say, 'Mummy's coffee's hot. Put it up high.'

More to say: ideas for parents

- **Things can appear and disappear.** For early meaning categories, games of peek-a-boo will help your baby discover that things disappear and reappear – and this leads to the all-important categories of existence, non-existence and recurrence.

- **Over and over again.** Later on, your baby will reinforce these meaning categories by repetitive play, such as putting blocks into containers and tipping them out again – and putting them in again and tipping them out once again, and putting them in yet once more. You'll get tired long before they do and, inevitably, not all the blocks will end up back in the container.

- **Don't ask trick questions!** Do resist the temptation to demonstrate your child's brilliance by pointing to a sheep and saying 'That's a dog, isn't it?' with the expectation that they'll answer 'no'. That's asking them to deny something, and that's the most difficult of those important types of negative.

📖 **Talking and reading times**

Books are wonderful ways of helping children learn all the meaning types described in this chapter. Once children are old enough to listen to books like *The Very Hungry Caterpillar*, pointing out the caterpillar on every page strengthens both existence and recurrence. And books that have a particular character on most, but not all, pages, bring in non-existence as well.

Simple stories with everyday happenings are ideal. Your child will enjoy reading about things they do and see themselves. At this stage, they'll often really enjoy the *Spot* books by Eric Hill and lift-the-flap books.

Summary of tips

- Things can appear and disappear.
- Over and over again.
- Don't ask trick questions!
- Books are wonderful ways of helping children learn meaning.
- Simple stories with everyday happenings are ideal.

11.

Putting it together: more than one word

Twelve months to 24 months

Your child will probably start to put two words together between about eighteen months and two years, when they can use about fifty words. By then, though, you'll probably have lost count of just how many words they can actually say. Some children start putting words together as early as twelve months and others don't join words until they're well over two. And all are within the normal range for language development.

Just as it was almost impossible to predict what your child's first word would be, it's also equally impossible to predict what their first genuine two-word combination will be. And if your child babbles a lot to themselves as they play, it can be really hard to pick out their true words – whether they're single words or two-word combinations.

Two words together

It's breakfast time and Mum is busy organising cereal for three-year-old Lucy when twelve-month-old David announces firmly, 'Nana Dadid!' 'Nana' (banana) is his word for food, and 'Dadid' is how he says his name. So David is saying 'Feed *me!*'

Twenty-two-month-old Harry says, 'Daddy bye-bye' as he hears his father's car leave for work one morning. That's the first time his mother has heard him put two words together.

These two little boys show that children start to put two words together at different ages. They also show how different first 'sentences' can be!

Simple sentences

As soon as your child puts two words together, you can say that they're using 'sentences'. They won't be sentences of the sort you're used to, but they're sentences as far as your child is concerned. We're not very good at identifying simple language. If you ask someone to give you a simple sentence, they'll usually say something like, 'The cat sat on the mat.' That contains a subject (the cat – the thing doing the action), a verb (sat – the action word) and a place (on the mat). Or they might say, 'The dog chased the cat'. These are common sentences, but they're not usually the sorts of sentences your child will use when they're first putting words together.

I'm always the subject!

For a start, your child probably won't use subjects in their early sentences. They're usually talking to you and you can see what they're talking about. So they don't need to say who's actually doing the action. Learning language is hard enough without adding anything that isn't absolutely necessary. And when your child does start to say who is doing the action, they'll usually use 'me' or 'you', or a name, like 'Mummy' or 'Daddy' or their own name. They almost never use two words like 'the cat'.

The things they say!

Mum said to Rory, 'Behave yourself!'

Rory was indignant. But instead of saying, 'I *am* behaving,' he said, 'I'm being-have!'

✣ What does science tell us?

New words for young and old

It's been known for a long time that adults use a special language, baby talk, when talking to children. One study showed that mothers tended to put a new or important word at the end of their sentences when they were talking to small children. Adults in the same study used a similar strategy for helping other adults learn new technical terms. A major difference was that the new words were spoken on a higher pitch to babies but not to other adults. When words are spoken with a higher pitch and put at the end of a sentence, they really do stand out.

Names or relations

When your child starts to put words together there are two different routes they can take. Some children are fascinated by the names of things – they want to know what everything is called and when they put sentences together they use lots of these names. So they might say 'crash truck' and later 'truck crash car' when the toy truck crashes into a car. Other children are fascinated by the way everything holds together. Rather than using lots of names, they use 'that' and lots of words like 'in', 'on' or 'there' to show how things are related. If your child follows this route, they might say, 'That banged into that' when a truck crashes into a car, or 'Put it under there' to tell you to put the saucer under the toy cup. There's no way to predict which route your child might take, or whether they'll try to express both names and relations right from the start. At first, children who use the 'relations' route seem to have more complex language than those who use the 'name' route, but they all end up using equally complex language in a year or so.

Building sentences up

One of the special things about human language that makes it different from animal languages is that it has patterns inside patterns. Words are made up of sounds. So when you speak you make patterns of sounds inside patterns of words. Sentences are just the same. They also have patterns inside patterns. There are simple sentences like 'Jamie chased Zak', but you can make each part of the sentence more complicated and say, for example, 'The small boy ran after the bigger boy.' This is something animals can't do – each of their cries has just one meaning and they can't change them in the dozens of ways that we can.

When children first start to put sentences together they can only join up the major building blocks – 'Daddy get truck.' Or they make just one of those blocks more complicated – 'Big truck!' You won't hear them say, 'Daddy get my big truck.' So that's something to listen for. You probably won't rejoice when your child says, 'Want 'nother bickie' but it's a big step in terms of language.

> ## Humans are great at building patterns
>
> We build patterns inside other patterns. Animals can't do this. Human language can communicate so much because we learn how to make each part of the sentence more complex and so tell a 'bigger' story.
>
> Two-word stage: 'Pat cat.'
> Young child: 'Daddy pat cat.'
> Older child: 'My daddy is patting Monty cat.'
> Adult: 'My elderly father often pats the neighbour's cat in our backyard.'

Turn a blind eye to 'mistakes'

When your child is starting to put two words together it's important to turn a blind eye to their 'mistakes'. There are lots of horror stories about parents who try to correct their children's language. The linguist David McNeill tells a story about a child who came home upset about something that had happened at preschool. The conversation between the child and mother began like this:

Child: Nobody don't like me.
Mother: No, say 'Nobody likes me.'
Child: Nobody don't like me.

Then followed a further seven repetitions of this exchange, until finally:

Mother: No, now listen carefully. Say, 'Nobody likes me.'
Child: Oh! Nobody don't *likes* me.

Unfortunately, some people really do care so much about language that they don't listen to what their child is actually trying to tell them. In most of life, if you pile up negatives, it makes what you're saying more negative. Saying 'No, no, no, no, no' is so much stronger than just a single 'no'. But way back in the eighteenth century, scholars tried to make English more scientific and stopped people using double negatives. So today we say, 'Nobody likes me' rather than the stronger, 'Nobody doesn't like me.' Of course, Shakespeare cheerfully used double negatives. In Act III, Scene I of his play *Twelfth Night* he wrote:

> *By innocence I swear, and by my youth,*
> *I have one heart, one bosom and one truth,*
> *And that **no** woman has; **nor never none***
> *Shall mistress be of it, save I alone.*

That really does make the point very strongly!

Provide them with good models

There doesn't seem to be much evidence that trying to correct your child's grammar is very useful. But giving them the correct model without making a fuss about it can be surprisingly effective, especially when your child is a bit older. One day Matthew was trying to persuade his four-year-old son, Alex, to close the door because it was cold. Alex didn't want to be helpful, and with typical four-year-old logic, he announced that it was 'too *bored*' to close the doors. Rather than telling him that *bored* was the wrong word to use, Matthew just said 'it's not *boring*'. Somewhat to his surprise, Alex copied his word and said it was '*too boring*'.

Matthew didn't tell Alex he hadn't used the correct word – he simply used the correct word himself. And then Alex picked it up and used it too. The important thing seems to be that Matthew didn't *ask* Alex to use the new word and that he didn't comment when Alex did use it. It was all just part of the conversation. And Alex seems to have picked up the new word because it made his meaning clearer.

The things they say!

As Dad and Sonny walked up the driveway, the family's golden retriever came running to greet them.

'Look, Dad,' exclaimed Sonny. 'Rover's tail is flagging.'

What seems to be really important is to focus on what your child wants to talk about rather than on how they say it. Your child won't always pick up your model quite as readily as Alex did with his father, but eventually they'll hear you use the appropriate form often enough and it'll work its way into their language.

💬 Talking point

Your child says, 'Car break.'

You might say, 'Is your car broken? Bring it here. Mummy will fix it.'

More to say: ideas for parents ⚙

- **Model simple sentences.** By now, you won't be surprised when we say that the best way to help your child put more than two words together is to talk to them. Repeat back what your child says, but keep it simple. Make sure that the important building blocks of sentences are in the right order. If your child says, 'Tower … build,' you can say, 'You're building a tower' with 'build' and 'tower' in the order usually used.

- **Stick to the important words.** When you repeat what your child says, expand it a little. 'Daddy throw ball? Yes, Daddy's throwing the ball,' adding that all-important 'ing' onto the end of 'throw'. Or 'Daddy's throwing the ball to Sarah,' adding in their name. But don't try to expand too much.

- **It's okay to ignore the little words.** Stick to the main words rather than trying to emphasise all the 'little words'. When your child is just starting to put several words together, something like 'Now Daddy's rolling the big ball to Sarah,' with all the little words included, is probably too much for them to take in.

- **Two or three ideas per sentence.** Short sentences are most useful for your child: 'Daddy's rolling the ball. Rolling the ball to Sarah.' Or make it even simpler and just say, 'Daddy rolling ball. Rolling ball [to] Sarah.' Sentences like this without the little words still have all the meaningful words in the right order. And that's what your child needs at this stage.

- **Use your name and their name.** You'll probably have already noticed that you're saying things like 'Give it to Mummy' rather than 'Give it to me.' Words like 'you' and 'me' (or 'I') are confusing for young children because they change with the speaker. When Amanda is talking to James, Amanda is 'I' and James is 'you', but when James is talking to Amanda, James is 'I' and Amanda is 'you'. That really is difficult! When you use names, you avoid this hassle. One day you may suddenly realise that you're still carefully using names even though your child has started to use 'you' and 'me'. At that point, it's safe for you to use them too.

📖 Talking and reading times

Play 'fill in the word'. Lots of rhymes and early books are full of wonderful repetition. Incy Wincy spider climbs up the water spout. But he can also climb up lots of other things and the rain can come down and wash him out of lots of different places. Your child isn't going to worry if Incy Wincy has climbed up the table leg and the rain has washed him off inside the house. And you can pause after 'washed' for your child to say 'poor Incy out'. And again you can pause when the sun comes out for them to say that he climbed up the spout or the table leg again. When your child is older, they'll love to suggest new places that Incy Wincy could climb up. Of course, they won't be able to say his name very well at first but what's important is that you're reading a book together or just sharing the rhyme together. And as well as helping their language, when you use rhymes like this you give lots of space for your child's imagination to develop.

Read books that add words to a basic sentence. Rhymes and songs like *Old Macdonald had a farm*, *There was an old lady who swallowed a fly* or *This is the house that Jack built* keep adding items so the sentences keep changing and getting longer. They show how words can be joined together.

Make stories about your child's drawing. Write simple sentences or stories describing your child's drawing, colouring in or family photos. Children love to talk about the pictures they have drawn. You can also write a sentence or two at the bottom of the picture and read this back to them.

Summary of tips

- Model simple sentences.
- Stick to the important words.
- It's okay to ignore the little words.
- Two or three ideas per sentence.
- Use your name and their name.
- Play 'fill in the word'.
- Read books that add words to a basic sentence.
- Make stories about your child's drawings.

12.

Later meanings: expanding language into complex concepts

24 months to 36 months

Children can express many different types of meaning when they can only say one word at a time. But once they can join words together, the possibilities for expressing different meanings increase greatly.

Teddy Bears' Picnic

Lily was having a teddy bears' picnic. She set all her bears and dolls in a circle then went around giving each of them a pretend biscuit and cup of tea and saying, 'Bikkie for you.'

Even though she couldn't yet count, Lily could match up a biscuit for each of her toys.

'Quantity' and 'dative'

Matching up items such as a biscuit for each toy and actually giving the biscuits to the toys are two important meaning categories – the technical term for matching like this is *quantity* and for giving things to people is *dative*. Children 'perform' the meanings of both matching and sharing long before they can actually say them. A cooperative two-year-old will give a biscuit to Nanna and one to Grandad (so long as they also have one for themselves) or will line up soft toys and give each one a block to eat. What happens when two words can be put together is that they can now *say* what they're doing as well as do it.

Counting

Lily had cooperatively handed out biscuits to people for some time. One day, when she got to Teddy, she said 'Two bikkie for you' and gave him the right number – then, of course, she helped him eat them. This marked a real advance. She knew the word 'two' and giving Teddy the right number of biscuits showed that she understood the concept as well. You'll get really excited when your child can count to ten, but at first it's counting by rote – knowing the order of the words but not how to really count objects. Children usually know what 'two' means by their second birthday (two candles on their cake helps them) and 'three' by their third birthday (again, those candles are wonderful). Some, of course, understand numbers earlier than this but numbers and quantity are complex and we'll talk more about them in Chapter 18.

What does science tell us?

The importance of napping

Researchers found that six- and twelve-month-old babies who had a nap of at least 30 minutes after learning something new remembered what they'd learnt. The babies who didn't nap after learning didn't remember as well.

This shows how worthwhile it is to read to your baby and small child before they go to sleep.

Going where?

From early on children use place words such as 'up' for actions. Once they can put words together you'll hear action words such as 'jump' put together with place words such as 'up' to form 'jump up' or 'jump over'. You may hear 'fall over' quite early but it's probably learnt as a 'giant word'. But once your child can say 'jump over' then 'fall over' has most likely become two 'real' words as well.

Joining things up

It's snack time at preschool. Jemma has grapes, Jack has a bar and Sam has a drink. But Sam wants 'bar and drink'. You don't usually rejoice when your child tries to take another child's food. But when Sam wanted 'bar and drink' he was using a joining word, 'and', and that's a big step in meaning. It's the first step in joining two things together. Older children can say things like, 'I want to go to Jemma's house and play with her toys.' But before they can join complicated things like 'going to Jemma's house' and 'playing with her toys' they have to be able to join two simple words like 'bar' and 'drink'.

The things they say!

Anna and Peter decided to get married after living together for several years. When Anna said to four-year-old Jamie, 'Mummy and Daddy are going to get married' there was silence, then a small voice said, 'But what will happen to me?' It turned out that none of the married couples Jamie knew had any children.

Giving reasons

Soon after children start to join words, they start to give reasons. Although you usually use ''cos' or 'because' for reasons, that's way beyond your small child. Jamie always had his bath after dinner and then had stories and went to bed. When he was tired at night and didn't want to finish his dinner, he usually just said 'no' and threw bits of food on the floor. But one day he said 'bath'. And just to be more emphatic, 'Want bath.' He had figured out that if he had his bath *right now* he wouldn't have to eat any more food. That's reasoning, even though he's still a long way from being able to say, 'I want to have my bath because I'm tired and I want to go to bed.'

You'll probably have already noticed one of the most common early uses of reasoning. Your child will rub their eyes and say 'No bed, no tired' when their body language is firmly saying the exact opposite. They're not expressing their reasons in the same way you would, but there's reasoning there all the same.

Opposites

It's quite a while before children can express both ends of a comparison. They usually learn 'hot' before 'cold', 'big' before 'little' or 'small', 'long' before 'short', 'wide' before 'narrow' and 'deep' before 'shallow'. Before they learn both words in the pair, the most common one tends to be used for both ends of the scale, with some rather unexpected results. Jake was very aware that coffee mugs were hot. His parents were bemused one day when he complained that his ice cream was hot. Jake knew that both his ice cream and the coffee mugs weren't a nice, comfortable temperature, so they were both hot.

More advanced categories of meaning

These usually need more than one word:

    Quantity: 'two bickie'

    Dative: 'bickie for Teddy'

    Action plus place: 'run over', 'jump on chair'

    Joining things: 'teddy and doggie', 'bickie and drink'

    Reasons: 'no bed, no tired'

    Opposites: 'hot/cold', 'big/little'

Chains of meaning

Strange, unexpected results often occur as children expand their ideas of what words mean. Pippa's parents were somewhat taken aback when she pointed at the light hanging over the dining room table and announced firmly 'Duck!' Eventually they worked out the chain of meaning. Pippa loved the duck she played with every evening in the bath and she had a mobile of ducks hanging over her cot. Obviously, from Pippa's point of view, the hanging light looked like the hanging mobile and so the light became a duck.

A similar chain of meaning can lead children to call a dinner plate a 'moon' – both are round. Or the moon can be called a 'ball'. Chains of meaning like this can lead to lots of unexpected names as children sort out just how much individual words refer to.

> ### 💬 Talking point
>
> Your child says, 'Teddy bickie'.
>
> You might say, 'Does Teddy want a bickie? Here's a bickie for Teddy. Here's a bickie for you.'

More to say: ideas for parents 💡

- **Repetition, repetition, repetition.** You'll get very bored with repetitive play but it's essential for your child. Play is their work, and they really do work hard at it. But remember, this is something that your child does and while it's essential that you're involved and interact with them, you don't have to *teach* them.

- **Will it fit here?** When your child is a bit older, similar repetitive play helps them explore the more advanced meaning of quantity – how many blocks will fit into a box? How many can I stack to make a tower? Will this big block fit into this little box? As they learn the meaning 'quantity', they're also learning the idea of volume. A block is the same size whatever way you try to put it into a box – if the block is bigger than the box, it just won't fit!

- **Comment, comment, comment.** As usual, commenting on what your child is doing is important for these more complex types of meaning. 'You're climbing on the chair. Jumping off. Now you're up again.' And when they have still more words, actually commenting on the most complex types of meaning is just as important: 'You need to have your coat on because it's cold,' or 'Look, there's a big dog and a little dog.'

📖 Talking and reading times

Read simple counting books like *Ten Little Fingers and Ten Little Toes* by Mem Fox and Helen Oxenbury. Your child may not yet be able to count along with you, but they'll enjoy you counting their fingers and toes as you touch them.

Ask questions as you read together. You can use books to help your child develop these more complex types of meaning. You can ask questions like, 'What might happen next?' before you turn the page. Or 'Where might the turtle be hiding this time?' Since your child will quickly learn the answers to where the turtle is hiding, you'll have to be creative. For the most complex categories, like reasoning, you could ask, 'Could the giraffe hide under that bush?' and choose a bush that's much too short. Then when the child says, 'No!' you can ask, 'Why not?' and eventually the child will be able to give you a reason like, 'The giraffe is big and the bush is small,' which combines a joining word (and) with opposites (big and small). However, don't be in a rush – it's a long time before children are able to provide complex answers like this. Books will help your child develop concepts all through their preschool years. They keep helping us beyond school days and we can still learn new words and meanings from books throughout our life.

Use the book to talk about your child's wider world. As you read together, comment on where your child has seen or done the things in the story.

Enjoy more complex pictures. Books with many pictures on each page are also very good when your child is learning more complex types of meaning. Richard Scarry's books, which have many different vehicles on a page, or lots of people doing different kinds of work, are really helpful. Popular titles include *Best Word Book Ever, Cars, Trucks and Things that Go; A Day at the Airport;* and *What do People do all Day?* The pictures are relatively simple but there are lots of things that children recognise and the same 'people' appear on the different pages, letting you ask all sorts of questions that will help your child explore all sorts of more complex meanings.

Summary of tips

- Repetition, repetition, repetition.
- Will it fit here?
- Comment, comment, comment.
- Read simple counting books.
- Ask questions as you read together.
- Use the book to talk about your child's wider world.
- Enjoy more complex pictures.

13.

Listen to what I can say: early sound development

Nine months to three years

Vowel sounds are easy to say – and so your child will say them first. The earliest vowel your baby is likely to use is the 'aa' sound (as in the word 'car'). You've already heard them say that in their early babble – 'bababa', 'mamama', 'dadada' – and they'll probably just continue to use it when they start to make words. Then the other vowels slowly develop. When we think of vowels, we usually think of the five vowels we use when writing: A, E, I, O, U. But most varieties of English actually have about eighteen different vowel sounds so your baby has to learn a lot more than just five.

Don't worry if your baby sometimes sounds as though they have a bit of a strange accent. We don't know why some babies make some of the vowels a bit strangely. By the time they're putting two words together, any 'foreign accent' has usually disappeared.

The speed of speech

When we speak at a normal rate, we use as many as ten sounds in a second or 600 sounds in a minute. That's a lot!

Beyond vowels: early consonants

When we think of consonants, we usually think of writing and the letters of the alphabet. But again, English has more consonant sounds than we have letters to use to write them. English actually has 24 different consonant sounds so some of them, like 'sh' or 'th', are usually spelt with two letters. And just to make things difficult for us when we try to match letters and sounds, some letters make different sounds in different words. For example, 'c' sometimes sounds like a 'k' – as in cat – and sometimes like an 's' – as in city.

The things they say!

Cory adored all aeroplanes. One day he pointed to the sky and said, 'Look! A helipopter!'

There's a lot of variation in the ages at which children learn to produce consonant sounds, just as there's variation in the age when they start to walk or climb or when they're toilet trained. Children can easily learn sounds six months earlier or later than the ages given in developmental tables. So if your child isn't making a given sound at the suggested age, there's plenty of scope for it to develop a bit later.

Your child will probably be able to say 'm', 'n', 'p', 'b', 'h', 'w' and 'f' by about three years. They may also be using 't' or 'd' by then. By four years their number of sounds will probably have grown so they can also produce 'k' (often spelt with a 'c' as in 'cat'), 'g' (as in 'go' or 'goat'), 'y' (as in 'yellow') and 'ng' (as in 'playing').

Later consonants to learn

The ages at which the other sounds develop are much more variable. Some four-year-olds are using 'j' (as in 'jug') but other children don't learn it until closer to six. By six, most children will be using all the earlier sounds, and they will probably also be able to use 'l', 'v', 'sh' and 'ch'. They'll be trying to use the other sounds 's', 'z', 'r', 'th' (as in *thin*) and 'th' as in *that*) and also 'zh' (as in *measure*) but these are hard and children often take time to learn them and many are still sorting them out when they go to school.

Table 4: Typical age of development of consonant sounds

Age	Sounds usually used in speech
3 years	m, n, p, b, h, w, f, (t, d)
4 years	t, d, k ('c'), g, y, ng, (j)
6 years	j, l, v, sh, ch, s, z, r, th ('**thin**'), th ('**that**'), zh ('measure')
8 years	all single consonants and many groups of consonants

Learning one word at a time

When your child learns their first words, they seem to learn them one at a time. Each word is totally new – both in meaning and in the way they are said (their pronunciation). Sometimes the pronunciations are rather interesting, but usually you can work out what these first words are. But by the time your child gets to about fifty words, they won't be able to keep fifty beautifully clear pronunciations in their minds.

Early 'rules' to make talking easier

As your child starts to see patterns in the way words sound, they start to work out rules for pronunciation. These are usually rules that will make it easier for them to say the words. Unfortunately these rules often make it harder for you to understand them …

Your child will discover that lots of words start with a 'b' sound – book, ball, bye-bye, bus – and others start with 'd' – Daddy, dog, duck. And some words start with just one consonant sound, like 'book', but others, like 'block', start with two. It's much easier to say just one consonant at the start of a word rather than two! So 'block' often becomes 'bock' and 'blow' becomes 'bow'.

Using your voice

The first sounds children make when they babble are usually 'b', 'd' and 'g'. All these sounds are *voiced* – they're made with the vocal cords vibrating. You can check this by holding your hands loosely over your ears and saying 'b', 'd', 'g' and then trying 'p', 't' and 'k'. The 'p', 't' and 'k' sounds are *voiceless*, as the vocal cords don't vibrate when you make them. You'll hear an echoing sound with the voiced 'b', 'd' and 'g' that isn't there with the voiceless 'p', 't' and 'k'.

Your child will quickly decide that it's easier to make voiced sounds at the beginning of words and voiceless ones at the end.

'D' sounds galore

'D' sounds are heard everywhere in children's early words. Sounds like 'd' are much easier to say than 's' or 'sh', so 'd' often gets used in all sorts of places. 'Shoe' becomes 'doo' and 'Sue' becomes 'doo'; 'car' becomes 'da' and 'ta' also becomes 'da'.

At this point, your child may become very difficult to understand. 'This', 'fish', 'sit' and even 'bit' can all be pronounced 'dit'. The miracle is that you'll usually understand most of what your own child means, but strangers and grandparents are often left guessing!

⚛ WHAT DOES SCIENCE TELL US?

Crying with an accent

Babies cry with an accent within their first week of life. They cry with the same 'prosody' or melody used in their native language by the time they are only two days old. This was the astounding finding of a study of French and German newborns that compared the patterns of their cries to the patterns of their parents' speech. The melodies of French babies' cries went up, whereas those of German babies went down. These differences match major differences between the pitch patterns of French and German.

More and more 'errors'

When your child is learning how to say words, we again come up against that principle of early language development: an increase in errors means progress. Your child changes from relatively clear pronunciations of their first words to things that are much harder for you to understand. This shows that they're experimenting with ways to make sounds and words, and sorting out rules to make life easier for themselves.

> ## ⌐ Talking point
>
> Your child points to a dog and says, 'Bid dod!'
>   You might say, 'It is a big dog. That's Rover.'
>   Your child then says, 'Wower dod.'
>   You might say, 'That's right, Rover dog.'

More to say: ideas for parents ⓦ

● **An increase in errors means progress.** It doesn't seem very logical, but as your child learns more language there are more places where they can make errors. And these errors are, of course, indications that they're experimenting as they're learning.

● **Repeat the word back with the correct pronunciation.** The best thing for you to do when your child says a word incorrectly is to repeat back what they said with the correct pronunciation. And add a bit more, so that if your child points and says 'dod', you can say, 'Yes, that's a dog. He's barking.'

Sometimes your child will say a word correctly once and then go back to their usual mispronunciation in their ordinary speech. This is frustrating for everyone around, but it's very common and totally normal, so don't worry.

● **They won't imitate your pronunciation exactly.** It's really important not to expect your child to imitate your correct pronunciation. Usually they can't make that combination of sounds yet, and trying to get them to say something correctly can lead to a lot of frustration – for both of you.

● **Special pronunciations are okay at this stage, but don't copy them.** For most of this book, the advice we've been giving is just to talk. Copy what your child is saying and expand it, but don't try to correct them. Pronunciation is a bit different. When a small child says 'dot' instead of 'cot', they're quite sure that they actually said 'cot'. So it's not helpful if you repeat their pronunciation of 'dot' back to them – in their minds that's not what they said. So this time repeat their word back to them with the usual adult pronunciation, 'cot'.

● **Avoid commenting on how they say things.** The most important thing you can do for your child's pronunciation at this stage is not to comment on it. If possible, avoid imitating the child's cute pronunciations, although it can be hard to stop older brothers or sisters, or even friends, from repeating them.

Your child thinks their pronunciation is correct ...

One small boy was called John and like most small children, he couldn't say the 'j' sound. So when someone asked him his name he said 'Don'. Naturally the person said 'Oh, Don' and in frustration he replied 'No, Don, Donny'. The somewhat confused stranger said 'Donny' only to get more frustration from John. It usually needed someone who actually knew his name to step in before this was sorted out. John was quite convinced he was saying his name correctly, and imitating his pronunciation really didn't help at all.

📖 Talking and reading times

Nursery rhymes make for fun talking 'practice'. Nursery rhymes have lots of repeated sounds in them. They're wonderful when your child is starting to learn lots of new words. There are lots of repeated sounds and words – wonderful for practising.

Name pictures in books. As you look at books together, you can point out all the pictures your child knows the words for and say the word for them. They'll love to copy you and repeat what you've said – as best they can for now. Don't worry if they're still using their own special pronunciations – they will develop the proper pronunciations eventually.

Summary of tips

- An increase in errors means progress.
- Repeat the word back with the correct pronunciation.
- They won't imitate your pronunciation exactly.
- Special pronunciations are okay at this stage, but don't copy them.
- Avoid commenting on how they say things.
- Nursery rhymes make for fun talking 'practice'.
- Name pictures in books.

14.

I can really say a lot now! Later sound development

Two years to five years

A language expert was delighted when his daughter's first word as she looked at some flowers was 'pretty' (said 'pwitty'). Accurate and so clear. He was less happy a few months later when the flowers were 'biddy'. What had happened? Why had Hildegard's lovely clear 'pwitty' turned into 'biddy'? She still meant the same thing, so why was she saying it differently – and not as clearly?

Early pronunciation 'rules'

When we speak really quickly we can make up to 1400 sounds per minute. Most of the time we don't speak as quickly as that, but our tongues and jaws move a *lot*, so anything we can do to make that task easier is a good thing. And your child has to build up to the level of skill that you already have. So most children work out some predictable rules they use as they are getting better at speaking to make things easier for themselves.

Some sounds are much easier to produce than others so, not surprisingly, young children use those sounds a lot. One early rule makes most words start with 'b' or 'd' and turns any 'p' or 't' in the middle of a word into 'b' or 'd'. Another rule makes lots of words end without any consonant at all or with a 't'.

Another common early rule is that all words should start with just a single consonant sound – so the 'pr' at the start of 'pretty' is cut down to just one sound, 'p' or, even easier, a 'b', made just the same way but voiced (with the vocal cords vibrating). So when Hildegard simplified her 'pw' at the start of 'pretty' into one consonant, she turned it into 'b'. And the same thing happened to the 't' between the vowels 'e' and 'y' ('y' is a vowel sound here, even though we usually think of it as a consonant). It became 'd'. And so 'pretty' became 'biddy' – to her father's surprise!

Hildegard's 'rules' and those other children tend to use might not be our adult rules, but they make complete sense when you think about them as ways of making the work of talking more manageable.

The things they say!

Cory was so proud that he was old enough to get his own chocolate milk out of the fridge, which, to his family's delight, he called the 'freeridgerator'.

Time to be a detective

The 'rules' your child will work out make it much easier for them to learn and say new words. But for a while, you'll have to really be a detective to sort out what they're saying. And the more they can say, the harder you'll find it to understand. This detective work can be fun, especially if you can work out the 'rules' they're following. Let's now look more closely at some more of those rules.

Keep the 'b' or 'd'

Some words start with 'b' or 'd' followed by another consonant. Your child will probably keep the 'b' or 'd' and drop the second consonant. So they'll turn 'brush' into 'but', 'break' into 'bake' (or 'bait') and 'drop' into 'dop'. And words with three consonants at the beginning, such as 'string', are usually reduced down to one consonant at first and then two. 'String' becomes 'ding', and then 'dwing'.

Get rid of that 's'

Lots of words that start with two consonants have 's' as the first consonant: small, start, slinky, sky, snore. Your child will probably make these easier to say by dropping the 's' and then maybe simplifying the other consonant as well: 'mall' for 'small', 'dart' (or 'dar') for 'start', 'dinky' for 'slinky', 'dy' for 'sky' and 'dore' for 'snore'.

Half-way between

Sometimes the two initial consonants are merged into one consonant that is half way between them both. 'Swim' often becomes 'fim'; 'f' and 'w' are both made with the lips, and 'f' and 's' don't have the vocal cords vibrating. So 'f' is a bit like both 's' and 'w'.

Lots of trucks

Many initial consonant pairs seem to end up as 'f', including 'tr' (and that doesn't make a lot of sense, since 'f' isn't half way between 't' and 'r'). But 'f' instead of 'tr' is very common. Unfortunately it's often used by small boys who adore trucks and point them out loudly every time they go for a walk …

Spreading out: rules that cover lots of sounds

All of the 'rules' we have talked about up to now apply to one consonant at a time. But quite quickly, children seem to apply their 'rules' to whole groups of sounds. Now 'pot' becomes 'boh' and 'top' becomes 'doh' and 'cot' also becomes 'doh' and later 'goh'.

No final consonants

It's easier to make a sound at the start of the word than the end, so children often leave the ends off words. 'Jump' becomes 'duh', 'stop' becomes 'doh' and 'milk' becomes 'muh'. By about age three your child will probably at least try to put consonants on the ends of words, but at first they won't necessarily be the ones you expect.

Keep it short

It's easier to say words with only one syllable, so your child will probably shorten longer words. 'Again' will become 'gain', 'away' will become 'way', 'banana' will become 'nana' and so on.

Add a 'y' or double up

You may have noticed how many early words end in 'y' – Daddy, Mummy, teddy, baby. Lots of others double up – choo-choo, bow-wow, bye-bye, night-night. Your child may make other words double up – 'bobo' for 'bottle' or 'dada' for 'car'. Or they may turn one-syllable words into two – 'hidy' for 'hi'. This stage doesn't usually last long, unless some of the words are particularly 'cute' and the rest of the family adopts them, and you'll have guessed by now that this isn't really a good idea.

Use lots of 'b' and 'd'

It's easier to make sounds such as 'b' or 'd', where the mouth is completely blocked, than to make sounds with friction (a continuous stream of air) like 'f' or 's'. Your child may work out a rule that says 'replace all friction sounds with "b" or "d".' This turns every word with 'f', 's' or 'sh' into one with 'b' or 'd'. This particular rule makes many words hard to understand – it's the rule that turns 'fish' and 'sit' into 'dit'. Unfortunately this particular rule can last for a long time, even past the start of kindergarten.

It's not being lazy!

None of the rules your child uses to make pronunciation easier are due to laziness. Your child is still working on developing the motor skills needed for talking, skills that come so easily for adults. Most children are using the standard sounds for single consonants by the time they start school. Simplifying groups of consonants, on the other hand, can last past the start of school and still sort itself out without any need for help.

Harder to understand

The more your child says the harder they can be to understand. At first it doesn't seem to make much sense, but if your child is talking a lot and using a lot of different words they may actually seem to be speaking worse than another child who isn't saying a lot. This is because there'll be lots of places where the more talkative child can use their own pronunciation rules, and this is what often makes them harder to understand. As long as you can sort out what they're saying, things are probably fine.

> 🗩 **Talking point**
>
> Your child says, 'Deep do baa!'
> You might say, 'Sheep do go baa! What does a cow say?'

More to say: ideas for parents ⓦ

- **Be a speech detective.** You'll probably be much better at understanding your own child than strangers will be. For a while, you may feel as though you have to translate everything they say so others can understand. Until your child is about three, strangers will often only understand about half of what they say. You, on the other hand, will probably understand most of what they're saying, as long as you've got an idea of what they're talking about. By the time your child reaches four there's usually a big change. Strangers will probably understand about three-quarters of what they say – that's a huge jump in just over a year.

- **Let your child hear the correct pronunciation in a sentence.** If they're saying 'gog' for 'dog', repeat back what they said with a bit of extra emphasis on 'dog' so they hear the correct pronunciation. And it's good if the word is at the start or the end of the sentence so they can hear it more easily.

- **Don't worry about your neighbours' comments.** The most important thing with pronunciation is to get help if you don't notice change over time or if your child is worried about their own speech. Many people worry about the incorrect sounds children produce. But most incorrect sounds are part of normal speech development – children usually crawl before they walk, and so they make pronunciation errors before they develop the expected sounds.

📖 Talking and reading times

Play with sounds together. Rhymes, including nursery rhymes, are still really good ways to support your child's pronunciation. A rhyme like *This is the house that Jack built*, where something extra is added on each time, lets your child join in and at the same time gives lots of practice with the same words. Anything with nonsense words or sounds where you and your child are just playing with sounds is also really good as well as being fun. And a book with the words of *The wheels on the bus* (or other similar repetitive songs), lets you sing along together as the different things happen in the story.

Imitate sounds in books. There are lots of books that are ideal when your child is learning to make sounds. The *Hairy Maclary* books by Lynley Dodd, with their wonderful rhyming characters like Hairy Maclary himself and the cat Slinky Malinky, let your child say fun and different words, and repeat them often as the characters get up to lots of adventures. Some children love *Mr Brown Can Moo! Can You?* by Dr Seuss and other books like this, which focus on actually making sounds. The other Dr Seuss books also come into their own here. Not only are there wonderful things to find on each page, but the words are repetitive and zany. It doesn't matter if they're not pronounced 'correctly' – you and your child can have lots of fun 'reading' together.

Summary of tips

- Be a speech detective.
- Let your child hear the correct pronunciation in a sentence.
- Don't worry about your neighbours' comments.
- Play with sounds together.
- Imitate sounds in books.

15.

'No' and 'won't': Short sentences with a big impact

Two years to five years

You won't be delighted when your child firmly says 'won't' or 'can't' when you've asked them to do something, but in terms of their language development it's an important step. They'll probably be able to say 'can't' and 'don't' before they can say 'can' and 'do'. You've had to stop them doing all sorts of dangerous things, so you've probably had to say, 'Don't do that' or 'You can't do that' more often than you've said, 'Of course you can'.

One of the most important steps in being able to put words together into sentences comes when children learn the little words that help the main verbs – 'can', 'will', 'do', 'is' and so on. We need these 'helping' verbs to make all sorts of sentences. 'Can', 'will' or 'do' (or their negative forms 'can't', 'won't' and 'don't') are used in most of the questions and negatives we ask – 'Can I have a biscuit? No, you can't.' 'Will you please open the window? Why don't you do it yourself?' 'Do you want a cup of coffee?' And so on.

> ## The things they say!
>
> Sophie wanted to emphatically state that she could do something, but she wasn't quite three yet and what she said was 'I can't do that!' It was the first time she'd tried to use 'can' and the more familiar 'can't' slipped out. Fortunately, her parents realised what she meant to say and replied with 'Oh, you *can* do it – you *are* a big girl now!'

Learning to say no

As your child learns to say no, you'll see many examples of the 'rule' that an increase in errors means progress. At first, they'll just use the simple word, 'no'. Then they'll add 'no' to the start of the sort of sentences they're currently saying, so you'll hear something like 'No eat veggie' or 'No want bath.' At this point, your child is still talking mainly about themselves and what interests them, so they probably don't need to say *who* doesn't want to eat their veggies or have a bath. In order for negatives to develop any further, your child will have to put the subject into their sentence instead of just assuming you know who they're talking about. Once they can do this, they'll put 'no' in front of one of these sentences and say things like 'No me eat veggie.'

'No' becomes 'not'

The next step is that 'no' turns into 'not' and hops over the subject of the sentence. So, 'No me eat veggie' becomes 'Me not eat veggies' (and by now, your child is probably saying 'veggies' rather than just 'veggie'). This 'negative hopping' doesn't seem like a very big step, but it's important because once the 'not' has hopped over the subject, it can be added onto the little helping verbs. Now your child can say 'can't', 'don't' or 'won't' and they may even be using 'I' rather than 'me', so you'll hear them say 'I won't eat veggies' or 'I can't eat veggies.' Again, you won't rejoice when your child says things like this at dinnertime, but they're certainly doing brilliantly with their language development!

Development of negative sentences

'No.'
'No go bed.'
'No me go bed.'
'Me not go bed.'
'I won't go to bed' or 'I don't want to go to bed.'

What sort of question is that?

When you want to ask a question, you simply ask it. You don't worry about what sort of question you should ask. Most of the time we don't care that there are two different sorts of questions, but that's something your child will have to sort out. There are yes–no questions, where the answer is either yes or no, such as 'Do you like grapefruit?' or 'Are you ready yet?' And then there are wh- questions that start with a wh- word: what, where, who, when, why or how (how is a wh- word even though it starts with an 'h'). Examples of wh- questions are, 'What are you doing?' and 'Why can't I have another ice-cream?' although that last question is too hard for your child when they're just starting on the question journey.

Is the answer yes or no?

When your child starts to use yes–no questions, they'll use one word and raise the pitch of their voice on that word. When they want to ask, for example, 'Have you seen where the cat went because I just chased it outside?' they'll just say 'Cat?' Once they can join two words together, this rising pitch will go across both words, so they'll say 'Chase cat?' Next they'll be able to add both the subject and the verb into the question, but they'll still just make it a question by raising the pitch of their voice – 'Cat hide?' The big step comes when they can add one of those little helping words, and probably also add 'ing' to the verb – 'Cat is hiding?' or 'Cat's hiding?' Once they've got this far, many children want to make doubly sure that you know they're asking a question. So they double up the helping verb and say something like 'Is cat is hiding?' or 'Is cat's hiding?' Not all children do this, and they don't usually do it for very long, so keep an ear out and see if your child does it. Eventually they'll drop the extra helping verb, and your child can ask 'Is (the) cat hiding?' It's such a simple question, but it takes a lot of work to get to that stage.

What, where, who, when or why

Your child will go on a similar journey when they start to ask wh-questions. At first, they'll ask something like 'What?' or 'Wassat?' (and at this stage, 'wassat' is just one word even though it sounds like two). Then they'll add in a verb (an action word) as well and ask things like 'What doing?' or 'Wassat doing?' The next big step is when they can actually include the person who is doing something, so they can ask, 'What you doing?' And by this stage, 'wassat' has probably been dropped and they're just using the simple 'what'.

Answering the implied question

If the phone rang before dinner, Jack, aged nearly five, knew it was Mummy's work and he could go and watch TV. Suddenly, there was a clunk:

Mum: What was that?
Jack: It's all right, Mum.
Mum: Are you okay?
Jack: I'll clean it up.

When she got off the phone, Mummy discovered that Jack had dropped the jam while making himself a sandwich. Fortunately the jar was plastic, and he had, almost, cleaned it up. And Jack had realised that his mother's first question was really asking if he had hurt himself.

When children start to use the little helping verbs, they'll first put them in their usual place just in front of the main verb – 'What you are doing?' or 'What you're doing?' And, as with negatives, some children want to make doubly sure that you know they're asking a question so they double up on the helping verbs. You may be lucky enough to hear your child ask, 'What are you are doing?' or 'What are you're doing?' Not all children do this, and they don't usually do it for very long, but it's fun if you do hear questions like this because they show that your child really is working on the rules of language! Finally, the extra helping verb drops out and your child can actually ask, 'What are you doing?'

It's amazing that some children can use the same forms of questions and negatives as you do by the time they're three years old. Lots of other children take quite a bit longer to get there, but get there they do.

Development of questions

Bickie?	Where?
Me bickie?	Where go?
Me have bickie?	Where you go?
Me can have bickie?	Where you are going?
Can I can have a bickie?	Where are you are going?
Can I have a bickie?	Where are you going?

Answering questions

Another thing your child will need to learn is how to answer questions, especially those you'll ask when you don't understand what they just said. At first, if you ask your child to explain what they said, they'll totally ignore you. But some time between ages two and three they'll try to answer. At first they'll repeat exactly what they just said, only louder. You might find this helpful if you didn't hear because of noise, but it doesn't usually help a lot. Slowly, your child will learn to change what they just said in a more helpful way. It's a long time before they can really rephrase their questions, but at least by about age three they'll try, and that's a step in the right direction.

💬 Talking point

Your child says, 'Me no sleep.'
    You might say, 'I think you are sleepy. Time for a nap.'

Your child points to a cat in a picture and says, 'Cat. Out.'
    You might say, 'Where's the cat? Cat's gone outside. Bye-bye cat.'

More to say: ideas for parents ⚲

- **Listen for doubling up.** You're probably so busy working out what your child is saying that it can be hard to focus on *how* they're saying it. Your child may double up on the helping verbs or the negatives for a short time and say things like, 'No me not go bed' or 'Where's Rover's going?' These double-ups really show that your child is working on the rules of language, so it's good to notice them if you can – and then without any fuss provide the appropriate model: 'Where's Rover going? He's going outside.' Or 'You don't want to go to bed. Well it really is bedtime …'

- **Keep your own questions simple.** Some question words are harder for your child to understand than others. 'What' and 'where' are the easiest wh- questions to understand, so at first stick to questions like, 'What are they doing?' or 'Where is the dog going next?' and try to avoid ones that start with 'why'.

📖 Talking and reading times

Re-read favourite books. Your child will rapidly develop favourite books and they'll want you to read and re-read them every day. This provides a perfect opportunity for you to ask questions and then to let your child ask you questions. Because you both know the book so well, you can ask what's on the next page or who is going to appear next.

Books with flaps are wonderful. Books with flaps that can be lifted so you can see what is underneath are wonderful when your child is starting to use questions and working out how to say no. You can ask *what* is hiding under the flap, or *where* the ball is going to be hiding next. And when your child is a bit older, you can make silly suggestions like, 'The ball is hiding under the table' when you both know it's hiding behind the door. Your child will be delighted to correct you.

Summary of tips

- Listen for doubling up.
- Keep your own questions simple.
- Re-read favourite books.
- Books with flaps are wonderful.

16.

The three 'terrible question' stages

Two years to five years

Over and over again

Anna was exhausted. Mia wasn't quite two yet but she was talking non-stop. Her current favourite word was 'Wassat?' Anna would patiently answer, 'It's your rabbit' only to have Mia immediately ask 'Wassat?' again and point to her rabbit once more. After four or five repetitions of this, Anna was ready to tear her hair out. When she finally said, 'You know what it is. What is it? You tell me,' Mia happily said, 'Rabbit'.

Somewhere along the line, your child will probably start to ask 'Wassat?' when they already know the names of things, and you may well feel you're getting to the end of your tether. Lots of children go through three really frustrating stages as they learn to ask questions. You probably already know about the 'why' questions, but you may not know about the other two stages, and all three can be so frustrating for you and everyone else around your child.

What's that?

The first terrible question is 'What's that?' It sounds totally innocent, and if you ask it you want a literal answer – 'It's a tool to fix my car with' or whatever the correct answer is. But if your child points to a table and says 'What's that?' and you answer, 'It's a table,' they'll probably simply ask, 'What's that?' all over again, and again. Very frustrating, especially if they already know what it's called. This 'What's that?' stage usually happens when your child is about twenty months old. And this means, of course, that it can happen when your child is anywhere from about fourteen months to 26 months, or even slightly older.

What seems to be happening in the 'What's that?' stage is that your child is checking out that they really do know the names of things. And the 'correct' answer for you to give is usually, 'Well, what is it? You tell me.'

And with great triumph, your child will say 'table' or 'duck' or 'teddy bear'. And then the game goes on again. But having established that they did know the word, this time your child will usually move on to asking 'What's that?' about something different. It can be a wonderful relief to frustrated parents to discover the 'correct' way of answering these 'What's that?' questions. Neither you, nor your child, is going mad!

Why?

The second terrible question is the only one that most people know about: 'Why?' Your child will probably start to ask it somewhere between three-and-a-half and four years of age. At first they won't fully understand what 'why' means and they'll ask a question like, 'Why is the tree?' that really doesn't have a sensible answer.

But once your child discovers what 'why' means, they'll want you to give them a reason. Chains of 'why' questions can go on for a very long time. 'Why do I have to get dressed?' 'Because we're going to Nanna's.' 'Why are we going to Nanna's?' 'Because it's Saturday, and we always go to Nanna's on Saturday.' 'But why are we going on Saturday?' 'So Daddy can come with us.' 'Why can Daddy come with us?' 'He's not working today – today's Saturday and Daddy doesn't work on Saturday.' 'Why doesn't Daddy work on Saturday?' And so it goes on, for as long as you're willing to answer.

If you're like most parents, you'll eventually get tired of 'why' questions and you'll tell your child to stop asking them. But hopefully, you'll have answered a couple before you get fed up! Many of us work out a strategy to tell our children we're not going to answer more 'why' questions. When one of the authors got to the end of her tether, she would answer 'elephant's ears' and her children soon learnt that they had to find something else to say if they wanted to keep their mother talking.

What would happen if?

The third of the terrible questions is, 'What would happen if?' Your child probably won't start to ask this until they're over four or maybe not even until they've started school. It's a wonderful stage from the child's point of view, because you can always change what you're asking. Tom was fascinated by planes and parachutes. He'd regularly ask, 'What would happen if I jumped off the balcony with a parachute?' And the answer was always 'It's too close to the ground; the parachute wouldn't open.' So he'd raise the height: 'What would happen if I jumped off the second floor with a parachute?' And again the answer was, 'It's too close to the ground; the parachute wouldn't open.' So he'd progress to, 'What would happen if I jumped off the roof with a parachute?' And then to, 'What would happen if I jumped off Daddy's building with a parachute?' Daddy's work building was eight storeys high but the answer was still, 'It's too close to the ground; the parachute wouldn't open.' And so it would progress, always with something higher than the previous suggestion until his parents would finally say, 'You need to jump out of a plane for a parachute to open and you're too young!'

It's not about the answer

They're not really trying to drive you mad with their questions, although these three terrible questions really can be frustrating. And the 'problem' is that most of us are 'programmed' to try to answer our children's questions. We also think that if someone asks a question, they want to know the answer. So it's frustrating when you can't seem to give your child an answer that satisfies them. When you realise that what your child cares about is *asking* the question rather than getting an answer, you can relax. Depending on how tired or busy you are, you can play the question game for a longer or shorter time before you use your own version of 'elephant's ears' and close it down.

Which wh- word do they use first?

Even before your child starts to ask the terrible questions, you'll notice that they use some question words but not others. Some of the wh- words are a lot easier than others for children to use. Just as your child understood 'what' and 'where' first, so they will probably use 'what' and 'where' first when they start to ask wh- questions. So they'll say things like, 'Where teddy?' or 'What doing?' The next wh- word your child will use is probably 'who' when they want to know who is doing something. You can use this when you're reading a book. You can ask, 'Who do you think is hiding on the next page?' to help your child pick it up.

Time and time words are very difficult for small children. It will probably be several years before your child has a sensible idea about time, so 'when' will be a tricky wh- word for them to use. You'll probably tear your hair out when you're asked (again) 'Is it later yet?' (This usually means, 'Can I have a bickie or other food now?') Your child may ask, 'When is Poppa coming over?' but they usually have to be much older before they'll really understand your answer.

Even harder question words

'How' is even more tricky than 'when'. Your child probably won't use it until they're at preschool and want to know how to do something. But as you know, the really frustrating wh- question is 'Why?' Your child may ask 'why' questions long before they actually understand the word 'why', so they may ask questions like 'Why is the sky?' or 'Why is it Tuesday?' You can't give a reasonable answer to questions like these so why questions can be very frustrating all round.

> ## 🗩 Talking point
>
> Your child points to a picture of a car and says, 'Wassat?'
>> You might say, 'It's a car.'
>> Your child points to the same picture and says, 'Wassat?'
>> You might say, 'I told you, it's a car.'
>> Your child points to the same picture and says, 'Wassat?'
>> You might say, 'What is it? You tell me.'
>> Your child says, 'Car!'

More to say: ideas for parents 💡

● **'Wassat?' is a game.** Yes, you do need to answer genuine questions but when your child asks 'Wassat?', check if it's the 'What's that?' game so that the appropriate answer to give is, 'What is it? You tell me.' One small child used different tones of voice when she was playing the 'What's that?' game and when she actually wanted to know the answer. Her mother found this really helpful. Maybe your child will make a similar helpful distinction.

● **Think about the sorts of questions you could ask your child.** When we think of questions, we usually think of 'Why?' and that's one of the last questions children can really understand. When you're out walking with your child or reading a book together, ask lots of the earlier questions: 'Who is doing that?' 'Where is the dog going?' 'What is that man making?' Until your child is aged nearly four years, avoid asking 'How will the fireman get to his truck?' or 'Why is the baby crying?'

♥ **It's okay to set limits on answering questions.** Most of us have been brought up to be 'polite' and answer all the questions we're asked. But children at the question-asking stage ask questions for the sheer delight of asking questions. Answer as many as you can so your child gets practice in talking with you, but you don't have to answer everything they ask. To stay sane, you'll probably need to work out a way to let your child know you've had enough of the question game for now – but you'll play with them again later, next time you read a book together.

📖 Talking and reading times

Ask questions as you read together. Books like Mercer Mayer's *Frog, Where Are You?* provide the perfect opportunity to ask 'Where is the frog hiding this time?' and practise the relatively simple 'where' questions. After a while, your child can ask you the question and you can guess sensible or silly places. And books like Richard Scarry's *What Do People Do All Day?* let you ask about *who* is doing something, *where* they are, *what* they are doing and, when your child is older, even *why* they're doing it. You'll soon find your favourite books for reading together.

Books with silly pictures are fun. So far we've suggested that you stick to books with realistic pictures because they are easiest when your child is young. But once your child reaches the 'why' stage, then books with silly pictures are wonderful. The Dr Seuss books with their crazy rhymes and zany pictures provide wonderful resources for both you and your child to ask lots of questions.

Summary of tips

- 'Wassat?' is a game.
- Think about the sorts of questions you could ask your child.
- It's okay to set limits on answering questions.
- Ask questions as you read together.
- Books with silly pictures are fun.

17.

Talking in the world

Three-plus years

> Elliott had been chattering away to his mother at the shops, but then she'd met someone she knew vaguely and they were catching up. Suddenly Elliott said, 'Daniel needs a new toy, Mummy.'
>
> 'Oh, is Daniel your brother?' the other person asked.
>
> 'No, silly, Daniel's our dog!' was the reply from Elliott, who didn't realise this person didn't know all the details about his family.

Putting the language jigsaw together

In order to learn language, your child has to learn how to put all its parts together. They'll have to have something they want to say. They'll have to know the rules for how sounds go together to form words and how words go together to form sentences. And they'll also need to know about how to use language to talk to others. They'll have to sort out when it's okay to say something – and when it isn't.

By the time your child goes to school, they'll have made a good start at learning all the complications of when and where they can say things, what it's appropriate to talk about and how they should say it. They'll also have started to learn how much information they should include. You've learnt not to give people too much or too little information when you talk. (The answer to, 'How are you?' is usually 'Fine' rather than a long list of your current ailments.) You also know that it's not usually appropriate to tell people things you know aren't true or to give answers that are way off topic. And finally, you know not to make your answers ambiguous – not to drown your listeners in big words or give instructions out of order.

But by the time your child starts school they'll still be learning some of these 'rules', especially the rule about not getting things out of order. They'll have learnt so much, but there's still more to learn.

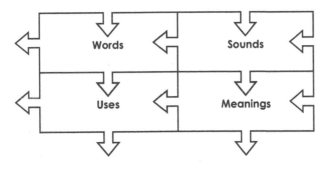

The language jigsaw

Different ways of talking in different situations

Up to about age three, your child will talk to everyone in the same way. But between three and four years of age, things change. Most of us seem to automatically use simpler language when we speak to small babies. And by age four, children use this 'baby talk' to babies just as their parents do. One afternoon Becky told her mother, 'Daddy's lying down on the bed, he must be tired.' A few minutes later, Becky told her little sister, 'Shh! Daddy gone night-night.'

Somewhere between three and four, your child will also learn which words they can and can't use where. If you don't use swear words, you probably won't be delighted if your child suddenly starts to use them. One day Fraser used several swear words from the safety of the other side of the slide in the local playground, where he knew his mother could hear him but couldn't reach him. Instead of reacting (with either outrage or laughter), his mother completely ignored him and the forbidden words lost their shock value. But she did wonder where he'd picked them up and how he knew to avoid her as he used them … On a more positive note, your child may start to say 'please' and 'thank you' without too much prompting and to speak quietly inside the house rather than shouting as they do outside.

Hinting and being diplomatic

You're probably like most parents: you want your child to be direct and not use hints. This is wonderful in theory, but the problem is that we use lots of hints when we want to be polite. You've probably said, 'I'm cold' rather than 'Please shut the door.' If we spent all our time using direct language – 'Give me a biscuit', 'Open that window', 'Make a cup of coffee' – we'd be very abrupt and rub people up the wrong way. So we fudge things – 'Would you mind shutting that door?' 'I'd really like a cup of coffee if it's no trouble.' Or we use hints – 'It's getting rather cold' (please shut the door), 'I'm really thirsty' (what about making some coffee?). At first, your child will ask very directly for what they want. They'll start by holding out their hand or pointing. Then they'll progress to 'bickie' or 'ball'. But by the time they're about three, they'll start to be more diplomatic.

Barking for biscuits

Three-year-old Sarah had enjoyed watching the keepers feed the seals at the local zoo, and had noticed how the seals barked when they thought it was their turn for a fish. The next afternoon, she crawled into the kitchen then pushed herself up on her hands so she looked like a seal and barked. Her mother was so surprised that she gave her a biscuit straight away.

Taking on a role

By the time they're about four, your child will probably really enjoy playing with other children. You'll notice them taking on different roles in their games – 'You be the shop person and I'll come and buy' or 'You be the mummy and I'll be the daddy and Tim can be the baby.' You may be amazed (or horrified) to hear your four-year-old using exactly the same language they hear you use at home. If your child is playing Mummy, they'll try to persuade the baby to eat lunch or go to bed. But if they're being Daddy, they may just tell the baby to eat without softening their request at all. Or if they're playing doctors and nurses, the doctor is often direct – 'I'm going to take your temperature' – whereas the nurse often makes suggestions – 'Let's just take your temperature now.' Your child will learn different ways to talk very early in their life.

Jokes

Your child may start to play with language and make jokes before they go to school. But lots of children don't understand jokes or puns until they're about seven. About that age, knock-knock jokes come into their own. Seven-year-olds love telling them and they get the point of the word play. Younger brothers or sisters usually want to be part of the fun so they invent their own knock-knock jokes – but these don't usually have a proper punch line. When your child is three or four they'll probably produce 'jokes' like: 'Knock knock.' 'Who's there?' 'Bunny.' 'Bunny who?' 'Bunny rabbit.' And your child will laugh madly and think they're so clever. You'll probably be tactful enough to laugh as well, but if they've got an older brother or sister they'll probably be completely unimpressed and even say, 'That's not a joke.'

Knock-knock jokes that seven-year-olds like

Knock knock.	Knock knock.
Who's there?	Who's there?
Howard.	Cows!
Howard who?	Cows who?
Howard I know!	Cows go 'moo' not 'who'!

💬 Talking point

By now you can have conversations with your child.

You might say, 'What did you do at preschool?'

Your child says, 'Played trains.'

You might say, 'Who did you play with?'

Your child says, 'Jack and Elliott. But Elliott wanted all the trains.'

You might say, 'What did you do?'

Your child says, 'I gived him one.'

You might say, 'Was he happy?'

Your child says, 'He was okay.'

More to say: ideas for parents ♀

● **Carry on talking.** As usual, the most important thing you can do is to talk to your child when they move into talking 'in the world' rather than just talking at home. Talk about anything and everything – your child will be curious about most of what they see.

● **Make it fun.** By the time your child reaches school age, strangers will be able to understand most of what they say, but there'll probably still be words or sounds that they find hard. When you play with your child, you can gently use these words, but keep it light. You don't want to make your child self-conscious.

● **Focus on what interests your child.** Playing with children, focusing on what interests them, doing creative things, going to different places – none of these things specifically focuses on language, but they will all help your child to learn – and that will help their language skills to develop.

● **'Review' your child's day together.** Tea time or bath time gives a good opportunity to talk about the things your child has done during their day. You may 'lead' the conversation to start with but follow up anything your child says with a comment or two. These conversations build language and also help your child form memories about their daily life.

📖 Talking and reading times

They'll want to read to you. By the time your child starts school they'll have a good idea about books. They'll know which way up to hold a book, and how to turn the pages one by one. They'll want to 'read' their favourite stories over and over again. Sometimes they'll want to read the book to you, but usually they'll want you to read it to them. When you can no longer stand the stories, it's fine to strategically 'lose' the book. There can then be much rejoicing when it's 'found'. This repetition is really important for your child's language and eventually for the way they'll learn to read.

Letters and numbers may be interesting now. By the time your child goes to school, they may want to know about letters and numbers. They may even recognise words they see on notice boards or on packets of food. Some children, but not many, even teach themselves to read. Your child may be interested in 'reading' their name or naming the letter it starts with.

Talking or doing? Is your child a talker or a doer? Many children are so focused on doing things that they don't really care about books and language. But it's still really important that you read to them as much as possible. You may not be able to get their attention during the day, but you can probably read to them at bedtime. After a while, the problem may be to work out how to stop reading to them.

Summary of tips

- Carry on talking.
- Make it fun.
- Focus on what interests your child.
- 'Review' your child's day together.
- They'll want to read to you.
- Letters and numbers may be interesting now.
- Talking or doing?

18.

Language is needed everywhere

Three-plus years

Some children in Britain start school knowing 6000 words. Others know just 500 words. Some children in the United States hear 2153 words per hour. Others hear just 616. Who will find it easier to learn when they go to school?

Ready for school

Children who go to school with well-developed language usually learn faster than those who have to catch up on language skills as well as learn everything else. And language skills are essential for other basic areas of knowledge. Three important areas where language skills really help children learn are numbers, volume and logic or reasoning. Some children come to school or preschool knowing about numbers, volume and logic, but others have to learn the basics at school. School really is easier for children if they already know something about these three areas. We'll look at early development in each of these areas in turn and then talk about the development of colour.

Numbers and numeracy

Many parents get very excited when their children can count to ten – and it's a fun thing to do. Although saying 'one, two, three, four ...' is the basis for learning about numbers, by itself it's not all that children need. Counting from one to ten is called *rote counting* – it's something learnt by rote, whereas what children really need to learn is what's known as *one-to-one* counting. This is where a child can count off blocks as they say a number and put four blocks in one container and five in another, or can put three beads in one bottle and six in another. One-to-one counting is much harder than rote counting. Most children grasp the concept of two by age two, and three by age three (the candles on birthday cakes help).

Before children fully understand one-to-one counting, they usually go through a stage where they can match numbers. They can give a pretend biscuit (such as a block) to each toy that's sitting in a circle, or they can take several teddies and give one to Mummy, one to Daddy, one to Grandad and one to Grandma. Having people to pretend play with in this way really helps numeracy to develop. Before they start school, children are usually able to count one-to-one along a line of blocks. If the blocks are separated, it's usually easier than if they're very close together. And younger children will start off happily with 'one, two' and then count a couple of blocks together as 'three' and then maybe miss out one and the next block may be 'five' or even 'eight'. As children get older, so their ability to count one-to-one usually increases.

> ## The things they say!
> Susie was having a warm and wonderful moment with her little boy who had just very proudly turned three years old.
>
> 'You're my number one son!' she said.
>
> 'But my number is three!' he answered.

Volume

Somewhere between ages one and two – often around eighteen months – children start to learn about volume. It's very frustrating when children empty out all their toys and usually get bored before they've put them all back in the toy box, but this is the start of learning about volume, about what will fit into where. As they do this, children will often try very hard to fit things into spaces where you can easily see they won't fit. In a sandpit, they'll fill a bucket with sand and tip it into other containers, often trying several times to put a whole bucketful of sand into a much smaller container. In the bath, they'll try to empty a large plastic cup full of water into a smaller cup, over and over, even though it will never all fit. Or they pour water from a short, wide container into a tall thin one, and again are surprised when all the water doesn't fit – or, equally, when it does.

Once children can count one-to-one up to about five, you can put two lines of three or four blocks next to each other and they'll tell you they've got the same number. But if one line has bigger blocks and one line has smaller blocks, they'll usually say that the line with the bigger blocks has more. Or if the blocks in one line are closer together and those in the other line are further apart, they'll usually say the one where the blocks are further apart has more. Eventually, they'll learn to count rather than just look at the apparent size. All of this is learning about the way things stay the same size or volume (known as conservation of volume), and language is really helpful as children sort it all out.

Logic – early reasoning

By about age two-and-a-half, most children have sorted out the routine of their home. They know when parents go out to work or come home, when they go to daycare or preschool and even which days regular visitors come. When the garage door opens just as he's eating his dinner, Jake shouts 'Dadda' and he's right: Dadda has just come home. Somewhere around three years of age, children seem to put into words what they've already worked out – Grandma came yesterday, so today I go to preschool. We Skype Nanna tonight because I went to Aunty Janet's this afternoon (and we always Skype Nanna on the day we go to Aunty Janet's).

Children's early ventures into logic and reasoning don't necessarily match your own ideas. We've already met this when children start to learn opposites, and both coffee and ice cream can be called 'hot' because they're not a comfortable temperature. But sometimes small children's logic is just as good as yours. Elliott was frustrated because he couldn't push his new shopping trolley easily. When his grandmother looked at it, she realised that one of the wheels wasn't fixed on properly. So she said, 'Elliott, one of the wheels isn't on properly.' Elliott promptly turned the trolley over, worked out which wheel wasn't on properly and brought it to his grandmother to be fixed, pointing out the wheel that needed attention. That's very good reasoning for a two-year-old!

The things they say!

Jane and Andrew were in the process of buying a new house. Jane said to their son Charlie, 'We're moving to a new house soon.' Not understanding that 'we' included him, Charlie asked, 'Can I come too?'

Colour

Colour is such an automatic concept for us that it's hard to imagine not having the words for it. When you're talking to a small child it's automatic to say, 'Bring me the red block' or 'Look at the lovely yellow flower' long before children have any concept of the colours red or yellow. If you look at a bag of mixed blocks, they differ in all sorts of ways: some are bigger than others, some are different shapes, some have pictures on them and there are usually several different colours. At first, it's really difficult for children to work out what colour actually stands for. Is the block 'red' because it's square? Or because it's bigger? And why are those two very different things – a block and a book – both red? If the only red block in a set is somehow different from the other blocks – maybe a different shape or texture – and you always call it 'the red block' then it may seem as though your child understands 'red', but they may not be using colour to find the 'red block'.

In order to be able to learn colours, children need to know 'same' and 'different'. If you want to sort out whether children know colours, you need a set of items that are identical in every way except for colour – small square blocks with no pictures would work, or a bag of identical pegs. At first they'll all be the same to the child, and if you have one red peg and several yellow pegs the child won't be able to find one that's different and will assume you're tricking them. One day, however, you'll notice that your child is able to pick out the 'different' peg and then you can assume they can at least sort by colour. This does not, of course, mean they've got a fully developed concept of colour. It takes some time before different shades of the same colour are grouped together – blue and green are known to be difficult to separate. When he was learning colour, Jude went through a stage of matching colours. He'd point to two things and announce 'match'. And they usually did match. His parents were fascinated as he increased the number of colours he pointed to and the variety of shades of the one colour he was happy to declare as a match.

Which colours are learnt first seems to depend on the child. In theory, the primary colours – red, blue and yellow – and maybe white and black should be identified first. But that's not what we see for all children. For some reason many small girls like purple and can identify purple long before they know any other colours.

But wait, there's more

Between two years and starting school, your child will learn the language for many basic concepts that are important for early school success. *More* and less, *up* and down, *big* and little – children tend to learn first that member of the pair with more distinctive attributes. Basic concepts include location words (e.g. over/under), describing words (full/empty), number concepts (all/none), time (young/old) and feelings (happy/sad).

Early concepts

Here are some more basic concept pairs most children will know by school age:.

On/off	Front/back
Thick/thin	Long/short
Heavy/light	Hot/cold
Same/different	Top/bottom
Loud/quiet	In front of/behind
High/low	Above/below
Forward/backward	Smooth/rough

You can help your child understand how things belong together in a group or category by talking about some of the basic concepts together. You could talk about the different kinds of food or fruit or vegetables you bought at the shops or which of the different animals might belong in a zoo or on a farm.

🗩 Talking point

Creating an internal diary

Children can't begin to tell you much about what has happened, even what happened yesterday, until they get to about age three. But from about two years, they start to build their own memories of their life.

As adults we like to look back on key events in our life and we like to remember special holidays, birthdays, our early friends in our neighbourhood and so on. Researchers have found that we can help children build their memories by talking about their experiences. Talking about your preparations for an event and recalling what happened together afterwards is an important part of this process. Some examples might include:

'It's time to get the Christmas tree out. We always decorate it together. Last year you put the star on the top. That was your favourite decoration. Sammy's was the little toy sleigh. We put all the decorations on and then we turned on the Christmas lights.'

'You went to the zoo today with Granny. What did you see? Granny said there were lots of elephants. One, two, three, four, maybe five ... all with big trunks. You fed the giraffes some leaves and they crunched them. What were the monkeys doing? I bet they were climbing.'

More to say: ideas for parents ⚬

- **Use basic concepts in your speech.** 'Here's a *big* bickie.' 'That noise is very *loud*.' Give a bit of extra emphasis to the word. There are lots of opportunities to talk about basic concepts in everyday activities – when you are shopping, out for a walk, in the playground and so on.

- **Share their play.** Learning about volume requires things that can be poured, like sand or water. Play dough is another way to learn about volume. Your child can squash a ball of play dough into something flat, roll it into a long thin sausage or a short fat sausage. They can make it smaller, but the only way to make it bigger is to add another bit of play dough.

- **Comment on their play.** You can describe what they're doing: 'Teddy's on the chair. Now he's under the table.' As you build things with blocks, there are many opportunities for you to model direction words such as 'in', 'on', 'under', 'behind', 'on top of', 'beside'. From about two-and-a-half, children often enjoy playing with little toy cars, people, houses and farm animals, such as the Little People toys. Again, these give opportunities for you to talk about colours, size, number and other basic concepts.

- **Play simple hide-and-seek games in the room.** 'Are you behind the curtain? No! Are you under the table? No! Oh! You're hiding behind the door!' This game is great fun for children from about two-and-a-half, though children at this age will often 'hide' in full view so you need to pretend you can't see them.

- **Give simple instructions using basic concepts, colours and counting.** 'Pass me *two* pegs' (when hanging the washing).

'Get your *blue* jumper.' 'Put your toys away *in the box.*' Most children need to be at least three years old to understand instructions like these.

- **Introduce concepts through favourite songs.** Songs like *The wheels on the bus* are good for teaching concepts: the doors on the bus *open* and *shut.* The driver on the bus says, 'Please sit *down.*'

- **Opportunities are everywhere.** When you're shopping, children who are learning numbers can count apples into a bag or count the cereal boxes or tins of baked beans as they go into the trolley. Feeding the ducks in the park lets you talk about big ducks and little ducks, about ducks that come close to you and ducks that stay far away, ducks that are fast and get lots of bread, and ducks that are too slow and never manage to get any bread.

- **Explore the world together.** Watching a building site is often a delight for small children. There are lots of trucks and diggers, and maybe bulldozers moving round. Maybe there's a forklift bringing materials. And as the building starts to take shape, you can talk about what it will be used for – is it a house or a shop? What rooms might be inside it? And as you talk about what *might* be inside or who *might* live there, you start to explore possibilities with your child and help them to move from the actual building that is already there to the sorts of things that might happen as the building is finished.

📖 Talking and reading times

You don't have to get special books. There are lots of books designed to teach your child numbers and colours. But you don't have to get special books. You can find things to count or colours to comment on in most of the books your child already loves.

Notice shapes and sizes. It's usually easier to talk about colours and numbers than shapes. When you're reading books together you can point out that the ball is round and the sandwich is a triangle.

Read books that illustrate the basic concepts. There are lots of simple counting books with illustrations for the numbers one to ten, or books of opposites. There are board books and early books for children that introduce the concepts of colour, number, size and feelings. Bring out again the simple books your child has had since they were a baby and have them 'read the pictures' to you and with you. *Where's Spot?* by Eric Hill and other lift-the-flap books often also give lots of early direction words – 'He's *in* the box, *on* the table, *under* the bush ...'

Talk about the pictures in story books using concept words and ask simple questions. Story books often have great pictures with lots of concepts to model to your child. 'Here's a *red* ball. This one's *green*.' 'Can you see *five* frogs?' 'Where's Spot hiding? He's *behind* the tree.' 'These cars are all the *same*.' 'Which one doesn't belong?'

Summary of tips

- Use basic concepts in your speech.
- Share their play.
- Comment on their play.
- Play simple hide-and-seek games in the room.
- Give simple instructions using basic concepts, colours and counting.
- Introduce concepts through favourite songs.
- Opportunities are everywhere.
- Explore the world together.
- You don't have to get special books.
- Notice shapes and sizes.
- Read books that illustrate the basic concepts.
- Talk about the pictures in story books using concept words and ask simple questions.

19.

Questions and answers

In this chapter, we'll try to give answers to some of the questions we often hear parents ask.

Q: *Why can my child imitate a word accurately, but then he continues to use the wrong pronunciation in his speech?*
A: Children can often produce one 'correct' version of a sound when they imitate it directly, but then they go back to their usual pronunciation when they're talking. There's so much for children to learn when they're learning language that they can't concentrate on everything at once. See the next chapter for indications of when to get help with a child's language, including pronunciation.

Q: *Do second and third children talk later than first children?*
A: It's a myth that second and third children are slower with language than first children – this doesn't seem to happen till about the fourth child. Second children often talk even more than first children, because they have their brother or sister as a model and need to keep up with them. However, by the time the fourth child arrives the older children often talk for him or her.

Q: *Is it better to use grown-up language to talk to young children than 'baby talk'? Will this help their language develop?*
A: Children need to hear language at a level they can understand as a model for their own language use. So it's good to keep your language simple when talking to them, and using

simplified 'baby talk' isn't usually a problem. The exception is pronunciation, where it's usually not a good idea to imitate a child's cute pronunciations.

Q: *My eighteen-month-old child isn't saying anything. Should I be worried?*
A: Most children are speaking at least in single words by eighteen months, but some children who are really active focus more on motor development than on language. The most important thing at this age is to check if your child can understand what you say to them. Can they go and get something for you without you pointing at what you want? Can they do two things such as 'Get your ball and give it to Daddy', again without you pointing to the ball or Daddy. If they continue not to talk, then it's a good idea to have their hearing checked as a first step. Watch for progress and if your child is still not talking at two years or you are concerned, talk with your doctor or preschool teacher about your concerns.

Q: *Is it important to read to a child? What sort of books should I choose?*
A: Reading aloud is a really important opportunity for talking to your baby or young child. But with early books, and picture books, it's just as important to talk about the pictures as to read the words. See the comments in the 'Talking and reading times' sections at the ends of chapters 3 to 18.

Q: *How early can I start reading to my child?*
A: As early as you feel comfortable with reading to them. Research has shown that reading to children as young as eight months of age improves their language skills and that establishing reading routines from an early age is important for language development.

Q: *English isn't my first language, but I want my children to speak English, so I don't speak my own first language to them. Is this okay?*

A: It's really good for children to be exposed to the language of the community at home, and in Australia and New Zealand, that's usually English. But it's even more important for children, especially very small children, to hear you talking in a language where you're really fluent and comfortable. In most countries in the world, people speak more than one language, and if you give your child a good grounding in your own language they'll learn English at preschool and with their friends and other people, and become fluent in both languages. You hear more languages spoken regularly in Australia than in New Zealand, but you can't live in either country and not hear English spoken.

Q: *My two-year-old doesn't always respond when I call her. Should I be worried?*

A: Sometimes children are so absorbed in their play that they shut out everything else. But not responding can be an indication that your child isn't hearing as well as they should. If you're at all concerned about hearing, it's always good to get your doctor to check.

Q: *Why does my child say 'tooths' instead of 'teeth'?*

A: In English most words can be made plural simply by adding 's' to the end – cat/cats, dog/dogs, boy/boys, book/books and so on. But many common English words aren't as simple as that and have more complicated plurals – mouse/mice, foot/feet, child/children, tooth/teeth. These have to be learnt one by one, and most people don't learn some of the really different and difficult ones (such as cactus/cacti or formula/formulae) until they're adults, or even avoid using the plural forms altogether.

Most children haven't finished learning these more difficult plurals by the time they reach school. When your child says 'tooths' it shows that they already know the language rule that tells us to add an 's' when we mean more than one of something in English. They may even go through a stage of doubling-up the plural and say 'teeths'. This is all normal development.

The things they say!

One small girl, aged just over two-and-a-half, announced on her way to bed, 'Mummy, tooths is teeth, isn't that a funny word?' Naturally, her mother agreed with her. Other children are much too busy mastering motor skills – running, jumping, building, drawing – to pay this sort of attention to language.

Q: *At what age should a child be taught colours and counting?*
A: The concepts of number and colour can be learnt through play and through your comments rather than by direct teaching. But these areas are much more complex than they appear to us. They're discussed in Chapter 18.

Q: *My child still says 'waked up' instead of 'woke up'. Shouldn't she know the right word by now? She's four!*
A: Not necessarily. Most English verbs are nice and regular and just need 'ed' added to the end to make them refer to the past: 'Today I walk, but yesterday I walk*ed*.' 'Today I want toast, but yesterday I want*ed* muesli.' Other verbs change totally: 'Today we *go* to gym; yesterday we *went* to ballet.' Your child has to learn these *irregular* verbs one at a time, and it's hard to predict which ones they'll learn first and which ones will take longer to learn.

Q: *My child is repeating words a lot, especially when excited – does this mean he's stuttering?*
A: No. Many children go through a period like this when their language is rapidly developing and their thoughts seem to run ahead of their mouths, so they can't say what they want as fast as they want to. It is known as 'normal dysfluency'. Just talk to your child as usual and try not to fill in the words for them. If the dysfluency lasts for more than about three months or if your child is 'struggling' to get out a word, or is getting frustrated when speaking, it's a good idea to seek help.

Q: *Do I need to spend a lot of extra time talking to my child so their language will develop?*
A: Young children really benefit from one-on-one time with their parents, caregivers and other interested adults. However, there are many opportunities for language interactions that occur during everyday life including during changing, bath time, meals, walks or your usual outings such as shopping, going to preschool etc. Make the most of these – and if possible also try to set aside some special time(s) in the day when you can chat, read or play with your child.

20.

Is there a problem?

'Connor, no! My turn,' says James as Connor pushes in front of him and goes up the slide. 'He always does that!' says Jenny, James' older sister. 'And he never says anything! I'm going to tell his mother next time.'

Jenny, aged four, has plenty of language to express her outrage and seek a resolution and even James, at two years five months, is using language to assert his place in the world. But what of Connor? Is he choosing not to talk or isn't he able to talk?

How do you know if there is a problem and what can you do about it if there is? These questions are the focus of this chapter.

Is a difference a problem?

Children are all individuals and develop at their own rate. Some are early talkers; some are early walkers. A child's development often seems to occur in spurts with one area, such as motor skills (e.g. crawling), surging ahead and then another, such as language (e.g. first words) emerging. Sometimes there is a pattern noted across the family but often there is a lot of difference between one child and their sister's or brother's development at the same age.

Perhaps it is surprising, but often an initial concern about a child is rather vague and non-specific. Children are often very good at masking their difficulties by using the things they can do well, such as watching other children to see what to do instead of following instructions.

When to get help

Preschool teachers, doctors, and other education and health professionals make use of detailed knowledge about typical development or milestones. This allows them to make sense of how an individual child is doing and decide if there are any issues or if any help is needed. We've included a set of speech and language milestones in Table 1 (p. 2), some movement and play milestones in Table 2 (p. 52) and some typical ages for development of consonant sounds in Table 4 (p. 111).

You may feel – as a parent, teacher, member of the extended family or other interested person – that somehow this child's development seems different from other children you know. And you may wonder if someone should check it out. Sometimes you're worried about something the child isn't doing. This may be a genuine problem. But it could be something that children don't usually do until they are older, or even something that this child will soon do without any difficulty. Change is usually rapid in children who are developing without specific problems, so keeping a note of their progress over a few months can be reassuring.

If there really is a problem with the child's speech or language development, then early intervention in the preschool years is important and will make a huge difference to communication skills and readiness to learn by school age.

Hearing and hearing loss

Hamish is playing alongside some other children at a table with some cars. He looks up and smiles when the preschool teacher comes along but is silent. The teacher says that Hamish seems to enjoy other children and participates well in activities ... but there is something that concerns her about him that she can't quite identify. When asked about his language she finds it hard to think of an example of something Hamish has said.

Hearing loss is often a common contributing factor to problems with speech and language development. Often in children it is temporary or recurring due to middle ear fluid or 'glue ear'. But even a mild or fluctuating hearing loss can have a big impact as these early years are busy ones for learning. It is important to get a child's hearing checked if you have any concerns about it. Hearing should also be checked as a first step when a child is not developing speech and language as expected, even if the child has other learning or developmental problems. There are medical and other treatments that may be appropriate.

If a preschooler has a hearing loss it can be hard to manage their behaviour. They miss out on hearing what is going on or what they have been asked to do. Without this information they find it hard to do what their carers expect them to.

Signs of a hearing problem

Here are some signs that a baby or young child may have hearing problems.

- Doesn't respond to everyday sounds.
- Understanding and use of language is delayed for their age.
- Closely watches the mouth of someone talking.
- Inattentive, does not respond to their name or being called (toddler or older).
- Speaks very loudly or very quietly.
- Seems engrossed in their own activities and ignores other people.

Hearing tests

There are two different types of hearing tests and each produces a different result. A tympanogram shows how the eardrum is working and can identify middle ear problems, such as glue ear. Some family doctors do this kind of testing as well as audiologists. But a child can have a normal tympanogram and still have a hearing loss if the problem is in the inner ear.

Audiologists produce audiograms as a result of testing inner ear function. Some countries, including New Zealand and Australia, have newborn screening programmes to test the function of the inner ear and to identify permanent (sensorineural) hearing loss in babies, and start intervention early in life. These hearing checks are offered free.

Specific developmental problems

Some children are born with particular developmental problems, such as autism or a learning disability. Usually, these problems are picked up during the preschool years as the child's general development falls behind that of other children their age. The earlier these problems are identified, the sooner appropriate assistance can be put in place to help with learning. Typically, such children will also have delays in their development of speech and language and will need specialist help to foster the development of their communication skills.

It is important to seek advice to ensure appropriate nutrition and growth for babies or young children who have difficulty feeding or chewing. This may signal motor problems that could also affect speech development. Other problems, such as cleft palate and cerebral palsy, can affect early speech and language development. These problems are usually identified at birth, or soon after, in routine health checks and the necessary help is put in place early.

Does the child sometimes 'stutter'?

Many children go through a period when their speech contains repetitions of words or parts of words. Their speech can also be hesitant as they reformulate what they are saying. This is known as normal dysfluency. Normal dysfluency happens when the child's language is going ahead rapidly and their thoughts seem to be ahead of what they can say. It is usually short-lived and disappears over a few months. Just give the child plenty of time to respond and let them finish what they want to say.

Seek further advice if the dysfluency seems to be persisting, especially if the child is becoming anxious about speaking or you notice extra effort and struggle, such as pulling faces or foot stamping, as they try to get out a word.

For most children though, the dysfluency will be a temporary phase in their normal development.

Where to go for help

If you have concerns about a child's speech and language development or hearing, talk first to your doctor or to the preschool teacher. These health and education professionals will use their professional experience and training to give you advice about whether further follow-up assessment and possible treatment by a speech and language pathologist or audiologist is indicated. They can also put you in touch with relevant services in your area.

Resources
and further reading

The chapter gives information on useful websites, reading and books you may enjoy with your child.

Children's books

These are just some of the excellent children's books that are available, which we mentioned throughout the book.

Eric Carle, *The Very Hungry Caterpillar*

Lucy Cousins, the *Maisy* series

Lynley Dodd, *Hairy Maclary* books

Mem Fox and Helen Oxenbury, *Ten Little Fingers and Ten Little Toes*

Betty and Alan Gilderdale, *The Little Yellow Digger* series

Eric Hill, *Where's Spot?* and other books in the *Spot* series

Individual nursery rhymes or collections of nursery rhymes, some of which are available as board books

The Ladybird series of books

Mercer Mayer, *Frog, Where Are You?*

Richard Scarry, *What Do People Do All Day?* and other Richard Scarry books

Dr Seuss, *Mr Brown Can moo! Can You?* and other Dr Seuss books

Useful websites

American Speech–Language–Hearing Association: Speech, language and swallowing
http://www.asha.org/public/speech
The Association's official website, containing information on normal and disordered language and speech.

Caring for Kids
http://www.caringforkids.cps.ca/handouts/read_speak_sing_to_your_baby
An informative site on children's and teenagers' development and health prepared by the Canadian Paediatric Society.

Centers for Disease Control and Prevention
http://www.cdc.gov/actearly
This official US website provides information on normal childhood development and promotes early intervention when appropriate.

Home Speech Home
http://www.home-speech-home.com/phonological-processes.html
A commercial site developed by speech language pathologists with information on normal phonological processes (sound substitutions).

Kidspot
www.kidspot.com.au
www.kidspot.co.nz
A commercial website developed by the founder of *Tots to Teens* magazine and others.

Much more than words

http://www.education.govt.nz/ministry-of-education/
publications/special-education-publications/

A New Zealand Ministry of Education page that contains a link to the downloadable booklet 'Much More Than Words', with information on typical communication development in young children and ideas for supporting them. It was developed for parents and also health and education professionals.

New Zealand Speech–language Therapists' Association

http://www.speechtherapy.org.nz/page/find-a-therapist/
resources-for-families/

The site is designed for speech–language pathologists but contains useful resources for families.

Parenting Science: Baby talk 101

http://www.parentingscience.com/baby-talk.html

A commercial site developed by a woman who is an anthropologist and science writer. It covers a lot of topics related to parenting.

Speech Pathology Australia

http://www.speechpathologyaustralia.org.au/publications/
fact-sheets

This site – the official website for Speech Pathology Australia – is designed for speech pathologists, but contains useful pamphlets for parents.

Understanding children: Language development

https://www.extension.iastate.edu/Publications/pm1529f.pdf

This is an excellent simple pamphlet about language development written by Lesia Oesterreich from Iowa State University.

Further reading on language development

David Crystal, 1999, *Listen to your child: A parent's guide to children's language*, Penguin. This book covers a wide age range from birth to high school. It is research-based and very detailed, but contains lots of relevant information.

Matthew Saxton, 2010, *Child language: Acquisition and development*, Sage Publications. A more academic book that focuses on many of the issues in language development and goes beyond the topics covered in this book.

Author notes

Page 9. 'One of the best-studied and best-reported cases is that of Genie, the so-called Wild Child.' There is a lot of material on the web about Genie. One source is http://en.wikipedia.org/wiki/Genie_(feral_child).

Page 10. 'Families that talk a lot also talk about more different things. They use more varied sentences, a greater range ...' http://www.newyorker.com/magazine/2015/01/12/talking-cure

Page 13. 'Researchers got babies to suck on a dummy until they'd settled into a nice, regular rhythm.' http://faculty.washington.edu/losterho/Eimas.pdf

Page 20. 'Some parts of our language may have developed from birdsong – at least that is what some researchers think ...' http://newsoffice.mit.edu/2013/how-human-language-could-have-evolved-from-birdsong-0221

Page 22. 'Research into laughter shows it's not as much about humour as it is about relationships ...' http://www.nbcnews.com/id/3077386/ns/technology_and_science-science/t/#.VL7r4z_29hg

Page 23. 'There's a lot of research that stresses the impact of early language learning on how well children do at school. One study followed babies ...' http://www.ncbi.nlm.nih.gov/pmc/articles/PMC3262592/

Page 30. 'This was the incredible finding of a recent study using brain scanning technology. The study looked at ...' This research was carried out at the Institute for Learning and Brain Sciences at the University of Washington. http://www.sciencedaily.com/releases/2014/07/140714152311.htm

Page 33. 'A study showed that shared reading between parents and infants of eight months of age was related to children's language abilities at twelve months ...' Jan Karass and Julia M. Braungart Rieker 2005, 'Effects of shared parent–infant book reading on early language acquisition', *Journal of Applied Developmental Psychology*, 26(2), pp. 133–48.

Page 37. 'Researchers found that these children ... showed less brain activity and very strange behaviours when they were older.' *National Geographic*, January 2015, vol. 227, p. 76.

Page 42. 'Hearing "a lot of language" is positively related to children producing "a lot of language". This was a key finding of a study ...' http://eric.ed.gov/?id=ED449536

Page 50. 'Children's experiences at home are critical to early language and learning ...' Eileen T. Rodriguez, Catherine S. Tamis-LeMonda, Mark E. Spellmann, Barbara A. Pan, Helen Raikes, Julieta Lugo-Gil and Gayle Luze 2009. 'The formative role of home literacy experiences across the first three years of life in children from low-income families', *Journal of Applied Developmental Psychology*, vol 30(6), pp. 677–694.

Page 51. 'Interactive book reading has been shown to improve children's language ...' Barbara A. Wasik and Mary Alice Bond 2001, 'Beyond the pages of a book: Interactive book reading and language development in preschool classrooms', *Journal of Educational Psychology*, vol. 93(2), pp. 243–50.

Page 59. **Your child will probably have one or more words ...'** Herbert H. Clark and Eve V. Clark 1977, *Psychology and language: An introduction to psycholinguistics*, New York, Harcourt Brace Jovanovich.

Page 62. 'Research has shown that most eighteen-month-olds learn an average of two to five new words every day ...' This information comes from research conducted at the University of Missouri-Columbia and can be found at http://www.sciencedaily.com/releases/2014/09/140917141431.htm

Page 68. 'Halliday called these *language functions* ... ' The early functions of language come from M.A.K. Halliday 1975, *Learning how to mean*, London, Arnold.

Page 72. 'Researchers believe hearing less language in the home might explain some ...' http://www.newyorker.com/magazine/2015/01/12/talking-cure

Page 78. 'The sorts of things children can talk about ...' L. Bloom and M. Lahey 1978, *Language development and language disorders*, New York, John Wiley and Sons, pp. 382–3.

Page 80. 'Lots of interactive videos designed for babies and young children have characters who encourage the children to join in actions and activities.' http://www.sciencedaily.com/releases/2013/09/130924091802.htm

Page 80. 'Researchers concluded that if we respond to children ...' Sarah Roseberry, Kathy Hirsh-Pasek and Roberta M. Golinkoff 2014, 'Skype Me! Socially contingent interactions help toddlers learn language', *Child Development*, vol. 85, issue 3, pp. 956–70, May/June.

Page 85. 'In the United States, staff at the Gorilla Foundation taught sign language to Koko the gorilla ...' http://www.naturalnews.com/038743_primates_liars_gorilla.html

Page 92. 'It's been known for a long time that adults use a special language, baby talk, when talking to children ...' Fernald A and Mazzie 1991. 'Prosody and focus in speech to infants and adults'. *Developmental Psychology* 27(2): 209-221. See http://psych.stanford.edu/~babylab/pdfs/Fernald%26Mazzie%201991.pdf

Page 94. **'The linguist David McNeill tells a story about a child who came home upset ...'** The interaction between the mother and child is from David McNeill 1970, *The acquisition of language: The study of developmental psycholinguists*, New York, Harper & Row, p. 107. Used with the permission of the author.

Page 95. **'But way back in the eighteenth century, scholars tried to make English more scientific and stopped people using double negatives ...'** One of the most important people who tried to make English more scientific was Bishop Robert Lowth of London. He wrote about double negatives in 1762.

Page 95. **'One day, Matthew was trying to persuade his four-year-old son, Alex, to close the doors because it was cold ...'** The interaction between Matthew and his son comes from a public talk by Matthew Saxton, given on Wednesday 1 November 2006. The full text can be found at http://www.phon.ucl.ac.uk/home/dick/ec/cliemeetings.htm.

Page 101. **'Matching up items such as a biscuit for each toy and actually giving the biscuits to the toys ...'** The later meaning categories here were identified by Lois Bloom. See L. Bloom and Lahey, M. 1978, *Language development and language disorder*, New York, John Wiley and Sons, pp. 382–3.

Page 102. **'Researchers found that six- and twelve-month-old babies who had a nap ...'** Sabine Seehagen, Carolin Konrad, Jane S. Herbert and Silvia Schneider 2015, 'Timely sleep facilitates declarative memory consolidation in infants', *Proceedings of the National Academy of Sciences*, 112 (5), pp. 1625–9.

Page 109. **'When we speak at a normal rate, we use as many as ten sounds in a second or 600 sounds in a minute.'** http://www.psy.vanderbilt.edu/courses/psy216/SPEAKING.html

Page 113. **'Babies cry with an accent within their first week of life ...'** http://abcnews.go.com/Health/MindMoodNews/newborns-cry-accent-study-finds/Story?id=9006266&page=1

Page 118. **'A language expert was delighted when his daughter's first word as she looked at some flowers was "pretty" ...'** Leopold, Werner F. 1939, *Speech development of a bilingual child*, (Volume 1), Evanston, Ilinois, Northwestern University Press, p 70.

Page 153. **'Some children in Britain start school knowing 6000 words.'** For the British figures, see James Nottingham 2013, *Encouraging learning: How you can help children learn*, New York, Routledge, p 130. For the American figures, see Betty Hart and Todd R. Risley 2003, *Meaningful differences in the everyday experience of young American children*, Baltimore, MD, Brookes Publishing, p. 197.

Page 158. **'Between two years and starting school your child will learn the language for many basic concepts …'** http://www.superduperinc.com/handouts/pdf/52_Teaching_Basic_Concepts.pdf

Page 160. **'Creating an internal diary …'** Accessible information about auto-biographical memory that lets us create our internal diaries can be found in an article in the *Otago Daily Times* (December 26, 2014) written by Amanda Barnier and Penny Van Bergen from Macquarie University. More detailed information is available at http://www.psychology.emory.edu/cognition/bauer/lab/autobiographical.html

Page 166. **'Reading aloud is a really important opportunity for talking to your baby or young child …'** Some of the research that shows it is important to read to very young children can be found in Jan Karass and Julia M. Braungart Rieker 2005, 'Effects of shared parent–infant book reading on early language acquisition', *Journal of Applied Developmental Psychology*, 26(2), pp. 133–48. Barbara D. Debaryshe 1993, 'Joint picture-book reading correlates of early oral language skill', *Journal of Child language*, 20 (2), pp. 455–61.

Page 172. **'Hearing loss is often a common contributing factor to problems with speech and language development …'** These hearing checks are offered free. See also *Much more than words*, Ministry of Education, New Zealand. This can be downloaded from http://www.education.govt.nz/ministry-of-education/publications/special-education-publications/_

NB: All website addresses were correct at time of going to press. However, because they can change, you may need to search to find this information.